Study guide for
International Trade and the World Economy

AF719472

www.oup.com/marrewijk

Study guide for

International Trade and the World Economy

Stephan Schueller

Daniel Ottens

OXFORD
UNIVERSITY PRESS

This book has been printed digitally and produced in a standard specification in order to ensure its continuing availability

OXFORD
UNIVERSITY PRESS

Great Clarendon Street, Oxford OX2 6DP

Oxford University Press is a department of the University of Oxford.
It furthers the University's objective of excellence in research, scholarship, and education by publishing worldwide in

Oxford New York

Auckland Cape Town Dar es Salaam Hong Kong Karachi
Kuala Lumpur Madrid Melbourne Mexico City Nairobi
New Delhi Shanghai Taipei Toronto

With offices in

Argentina Austria Brazil Chile Czech Republic France Greece
Guatemala Hungary Italy Japan South Korea Poland Portugal
Singapore Switzerland Thailand Turkey Ukraine Vietnam

Oxford is a registered trade mark of Oxford University Press in the UK and in certain other countries

Published in the United States by Oxford University Press Inc., New York

© Charles van Marrewijk, Stephan Schueller, and Daniel Ottens, 2002

The moral rights of the author have been asserted

Database right Oxford University Press (maker)

Reprinted 2008

All rights reserved. No part of this publication may be reproduced, stored in a retrieval system, or transmitted, in any form or by any means, without the prior permission in writing of Oxford University Press, or as expressly permitted by law, or under terms agreed with the appropriate reprographics rights organization. Enquiries concerning reproduction outside the scope of the above should be sent to the Rights Department, Oxford University Press, at the address above

You must not circulate this book in any other binding or cover
And you must impose this same condition on any acquirer

ISBN 978-0-19-925314-2

Contents

Part IV **New Interactions**

Preface

You are reading the *Study guide* accompanying the textbook *International trade and the world economy* by Charles van Marrewijk. The objective of the study guide is to review and deepen the student's understanding of the topics covered in the textbook. To achieve this objective, the study guide provides a set of questions for every textbook chapter, subdivided into four different types of questions, as briefly discussed below.

- The 94 *review questions* cover the most important new elements of each chapter. By asking for definitions or explanations and by applying the theories to real-world situations these questions provide a basic understanding of the contents of each chapter.
- The 45 *empirical questions* bring the theory of the textbook to life by asking the student to search for data on the internet, to empirically verify the validity of a theory, to read empirical papers, and to find and evaluate real-world examples. Some basic knowledge of economic statistics, Microsoft Excel, and the internet is required for answering the empirical questions, that not only familiarize students with the available economic sources on the internet, but also give them the opportunity to undertake some basic empirical research.
- The 15 *simulation questions* allow the student to gain a better understanding of some of the theoretical models in the book. The Excel-based, user-friendly simulations can be downloaded from the book's website. They either repeat some of the textbook figures and/or show the numerical outcome of a model. Altering the parameters in red, changes the shown figures and outcomes. Analysing and experimenting with these changes provides valuable insights into the structure of a model.
- A thorough understanding of the theory can be acquired by answering the 17 *technical questions*. These questions usually review the technical notes at the end of a chapter. Basic mathematical skills (differentiation and optimization) are required for answering the technical questions.

Review questions and empirical questions are provided for every chapter. Simulation questions and technical questions are only provided if it is useful to do so. Simulation questions are included if there is a structural model to be simulated and the simulation improves the student's understanding of the theory. Technical questions are included in particular for Parts II and III of the book, providing the core of international economics, as the chapters in Part IV of the book present models that are too involved for asking technical questions.

The website of the book contains various MS Excel files with simulations and data (for some of the empirical questions). It also contains links to other information and useful websites for gathering (international) economic information (international organizations, data sources, etc.). In addition, instructors can download possible answers to all questions from the website, while students can download possible answers to the questions identified with an asterisk in this Study Guide.

Finally, we would like to thank a number of people, in particular Koen Berden, Teun Schmidt, Joe Francois, and Charles van Marrewijk. Koen Berden and Teun Schmidt have been our colleagues in teaching the course 'International Economics' at Erasmus University. We have worked together using a first draft of this Study Guide. Their comments and suggestions have greatly improved our work. Joe Francois taught us some valuable lessons in economic modelling. We would like to thank him especially for supplying the materials allowing us to complete Chapter 17. Above all, we would like to thank Charles van Marrewijk, the author of the textbook, for his support. It was a real pleasure working together with him on this project. His comments and jokes reminded us (sometimes painfully) of our limitations, and made us better economists in the process. We particularly appreciate his encouragement which stimulated us in our studies and in completing this (we think) challenging and interesting Study Guide.

Rotterdam, 1 October 2001
Stephan Schueller
Daniel Ottens

Note to Reader: Numbered figures, sections, etc. refer to the parent textbook.

Part I

Introduction and Classical Trade

1

The World Economy

Chapter 1 presents basic information on the structure and development of the world economy in terms of land area, population, income, trade flows, and capital flows. It also briefly discusses the meaning of some economic terms, such as purchasing power, the difference between domestic product and national product, and the balance of payments.

Review questions

Question 1.1

A. Which three conceptual steps have to be taken before we are able to give an estimate of the total value of goods and services produced in a country which is also reasonably comparable between countries?

B. What is the difference between domestic product and national product?

C. What is a 'purchasing power parity' (PPP) exchange rate?

D. Explain why the domestic product is higher for most developing countries if we use PPP exchange rates rather than nominal exchange rates to convert the estimates from national currencies to 'dollars'.

Question 1.2

This question familiarizes you with the concept of purchasing power parity (PPP) discussed in section 1.3. The PPP theory is derived from the so-called 'law of one price', which states that identical goods should sell for the same price in different countries, provided there are no transportation costs or other trade impediments.

A. What is the main economic driving force underlying the 'law of one price'? Do you think the law of one price will hold if we consider tradeable goods? How about non-tradeable goods?

B. Suppose that a pair of scissors is sold for 5.5 zloty in Poland and for $2.50 in the USA. At which exchange rate between the zloty and the American dollar does the law of one price hold for this pair of scissors?

The PPP theory applies the law of one price in the aggregate. In the absence of trade costs it states that the cost of a certain basket of identical goods should be the same in different countries. The PPP exchange rate is calculated by comparing the prices in local currencies of such a basket of goods and services, that gives a different calculated PPP exchange rate from the nominal exchange rate observed on the financial markets.

Imagine that Poland and the United States are producing and trading only two goods, microwaves and frozen pizzas. A microwave has a price of $200 in the United States and 438 zloty in Poland. A frozen pizza has a price of $5 in the United States and 11 zloty in Poland. Assume that there are no trade costs whatsoever.

C. Does the law of one price hold for both goods at the same time? Why, or why not?

D. What do you think will be the nominal exchange rate between the American dollar and the Polish zloty?

E. What is the PPP exchange rate between the American dollar and the Polish zloty?

Imagine again that Poland and the United States are only producing two goods. This time both countries produce a tradeable good; bottles of shampoo, and a non-tradeable good; haircuts. The price of a bottle of shampoo is $3 in the United States and 6.6 zloty in Poland. The price of a haircut is $10 in the United States and 15 zloty in Poland. There are no trade costs for shampoo.

F. Does the law of one price hold for both goods at the same time? Why, or why not?

G. What do you think will be the nominal exchange rate between the American dollar and the Polish zloty?

H. What is the PPP exchange rate between the American dollar and the Polish zloty if the 'basket of goods' consists of one haircut and one bottle of shampoo? How does your answer change if the composition of the basket of goods changes?

Question 1.3

The table summarizes Portugal's balance of payments in 1999.

Balance of payments of Portugal, 1999 (millions of Euro)

	Credit	Debit	Net
Current account	41,736	51,281	−9,546
Goods (f.o.b.)	24,097	37,384	−13,288
Services	7,859	6,366	1,493
Income	4,074	5,519	−1,445
Current transfers	5,707	2,012	3,694

	Credit	Debit	Net
Capital account	23,778	11,687	12,091
Long-term capital	2,464	178	2,286
Direct investment	1,044	2,880	−1,836
Equity securities	649	1,640	−991
Debt securities	10,792	2,846	7,946
Financial derivatives	2,517	2,332	185
Monetary authorities	471	1,417	−946
General government	−42	12	−54
Banks	6,474	−961	7,436
Other sectors	−591	1,343	−1,934
Net errors and omissions	0	2,345	−2,345
Reserves and related items	0	200	−200
TOTAL	65,513	65,513	0

Source: IMF (*Balance of Payments Statistics Yearbook*, 2000).

A. Is the balance of payments of Portugal equal to zero?

B. Does Portugal have a positive or negative trade balance?

C. Why does the balance of payments include the item 'net errors and omissions'?

Empirical questions

Question 1.4*[1]

Figure 1.5[2] of the book shows the relative exports of good and services for a selection of countries. The 'question 1-4' Excel file on the website contains statistical information on exports and income for many other countries. Use this information to answer the following questions.

A. Which countries have large export intensities (= exports/GDP)?

B. Is the size of a country related to its export intensity?

Question 1.5

In question 1.2 we discuss the PPP exchange rate, which is based on the 'law of one price'. Using this 'law' the weekly magazine *The Economist* calculates the so-called Big-Mac index, which reflects the exchange rate between currencies if the law of one price is applied to the price of McDonald's Big Mac in different countries.

[1] Indicative answers to questions identified with an asterisk are given on the website of the book.

[2] Numbered figures, sections, etc. refer to the parent textbook.

The 'question 1.5' Excel file on the website lists the price of a Big Mac in different countries. Calculate the exchange rate between countries based on the law of one price for a Big Mac. Compare your results to the actual exchange rates. Which currencies are most overvalued and which most undervalued?

Question 1.6*

The four graphs[3] for question 1.6 show the current accounts of several countries in the period 1981–99. Explain for each of the countries why the current account is either in surplus or shortage. You have to draw upon your general knowledge of the world economy to answer these questions. Chapter 1 does not contain this information.

A. Why are the current accounts of Kuwait and Norway in surplus over most of the period?

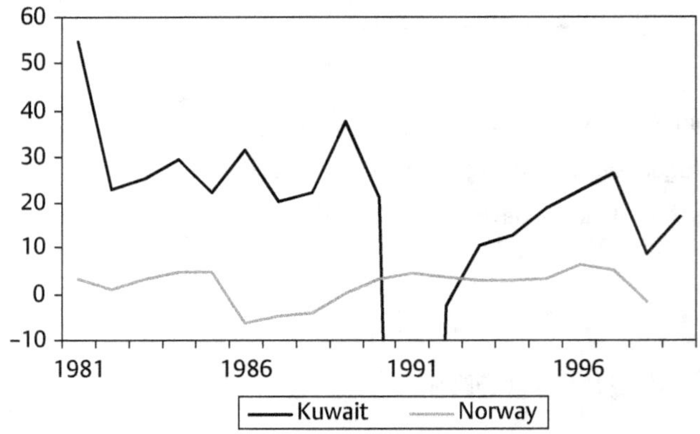

B. Why are the current accounts of Indonesia and Thailand in deficit over most of the period?

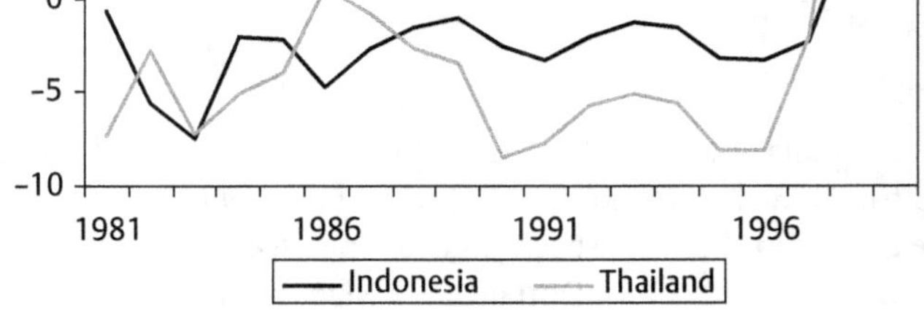

[3] Data are from the World Development Indicators 2000 (% of GDP).

C. Why are the current accounts of Belize and Antigua & Barbuda in deficit over most of the period?

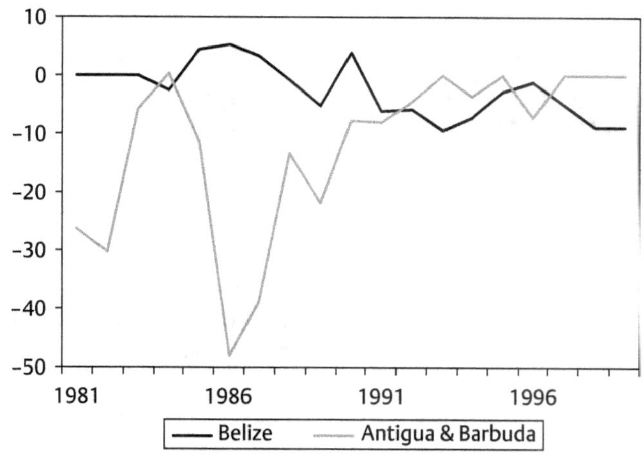

D. Why are the current accounts of Japan and the Netherlands in surplus over most of the period?

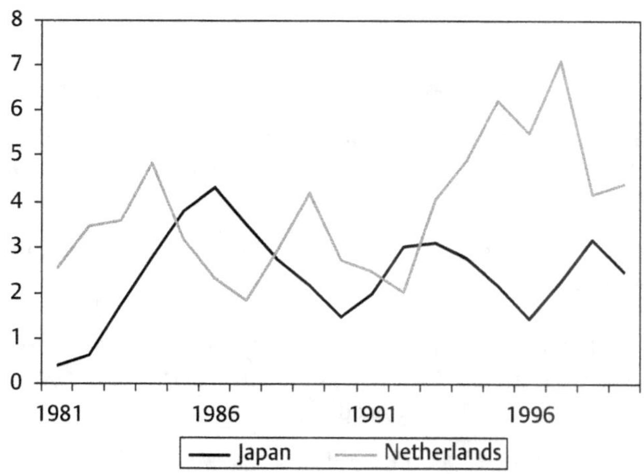

Question 1.7

Try to locate the working paper 'When did globalisation begin?' written by K. H. O'Rourke and J. G. Williamson on the internet at the National Bureau of Economic Research (NBER) website (http://www.nber.org). Licensed persons may download the working paper from this site.

A. What do O'Rourke and Williamson test in their paper?

B. How do the authors measure the degree of globalization?

C. What is the general conclusion of the paper?

2

Opportunity Costs

The classical driving forces behind international trade flows are technological differences between nations. If another country can produce a good more cheaply than we can, it is better to import this good from abroad. This will increase our welfare.

Review questions

Question 2.1

In section 2.4 productivity tables are presented based on empirical data. We will do the same in this question. Labour productivity in a sector is calculated by dividing total value added by the number of employees.

A. What criticism can you offer on this approach to measure labour productivity? (Think of the different factors of production).

The table is a copy of Table 2.2, which indicates the productivity of workers in the food and transport equipment industries of Japan and the USA. Assume for now that in both countries only food is produced.

Value added per employed person per year (US $, 1990)

	Food (311/2)	Transport equipment (384)
USA	82,337	77,582
Japan	48,273	81,928

Source: Van Marrewijk 2002 (ISIC category in parenthesis).

B. Given this information, can the USA and Japan both benefit from international trade? Explain.

Take both the food processing and transport equipment industries into account.

C. In this new situtation, can trade between the USA and Japan be profitable for both countries? Why is this the case?

Question 2.2

In 1998 one US worker in the tobacco industry produced $461,000 worth of tobacco on average, while one Japanese worker in the same industry produced $180,000 on average. Similarly, in the steel industry an average US worker produced $68,000 and an average Japanese worker produced $115,000.

First, suppose that the USA and Japan do not trade (autarky), that 45 people are working in the Japanese steel industry, 12 people are working in the Japanese tobacco industry, 50 people are working in the US steel industry, and 50 people are working in the US tobacco industry.

A. What is the total value of production (in dollars) for Japan and the USA, for each industry and country, and for the world as a whole?

B. If Japan and the USA traded with each other, which country would export which product? Explain.

C. If trade is allowed, what is the maximum value of world production (in dollars), assuming that all production will be consumed and prices remain constant?

Question 2.3

In a market with perfect competition and firms facing equal cost functions that are characterized by constant returns to scale, the price of a good (p) will be equal to the unit cost of production (c), see Box 2.1. Show this result mathematically using the firm's profit function given below (where 'x' is the quantity produced) if the firm's objective function is to maximize its profits.

$$\pi = px - cx = (p - c)x$$

Question 2.4

The table gives the productivity of American and Ecuadorian workers in the food processing and chemical industries.

Value added per employed person per year (US $, 1990)

	Food (311/2)	Chemicals (351/2)
USA	82,337	224,747
Ecuador	7,350	9,987

Source: OECD (*Foreign Trade by Commodities*), IMF (*International Financial Statistics*), UNIDO (*International Yearbook of Industrial Statistics*), ILO (*Yearbook of Labour Statistics*).

A. Will there be any trade between Ecuador and the USA in these two products, assuming that only absolute cost advantages can give rise to trade flows? Explain.

In 1998 the following amounts were actually traded between Ecuador and the USA.

Exports and imports: food and chemicals (million US$, 1998)

	Food (0 + 22 + 29 + 4)	Chemicals (27 + 50 – 57 – 58)
Export to Ecuador	146,756	2,108,363
Import from Ecuador	1,376,355	4,143

Source: OECD, Foreign Trade by Commodities (categories in parentheses).

B. How would you explain these trade flows?

Question 2.5*

The two graphs for question 2.5 depict the evolution over time of the Balassa index for the two industries with the highest 'revealed comparative advantage' (see section 2.6) in Germany and Portugal. Recall that the Balassa index measures the export performance relative to a group of reference countries, in this case the OECD countries. Note that the vertical scales of the graphs are not identical.

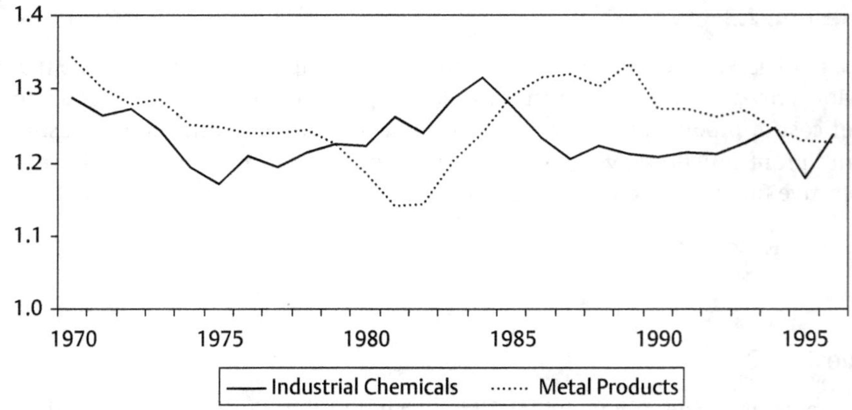

Germany, highest Balassa index

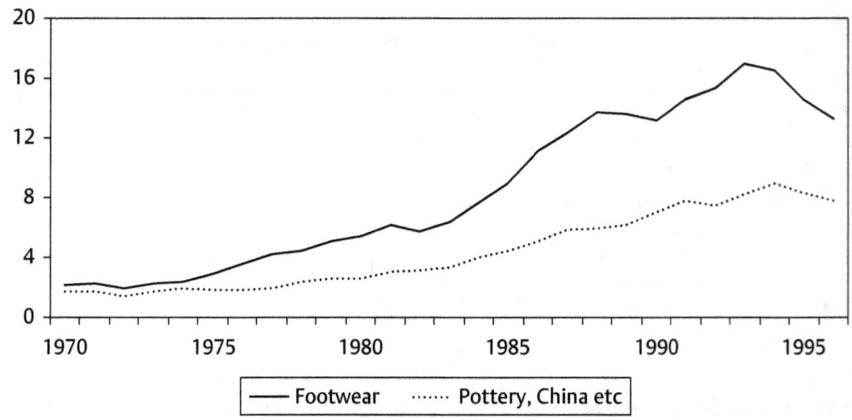

Portugal, highest Balassa index

A. Based on Adam Smith's theory of absolute cost advantages, that offers a possible explanation for trade flows between countries, how would you characterize the technological development of the industries in Germany and Portugal depicted in the graphs?

B. The Balassa indices for the industries in the Ottens (2000) study were rather stable over time (with some exceptions). Can you offer a plausible explanation for this observed stability over time?

C. The Balassa index is based on a comparison of *export* performances to determine a country's strong sectors. Can you think of some possible drawbacks of this method to identify a country's strong sectors? Explain.

Empirical questions

Question 2.6*

Chapter 2 argues that international trade arises as a result of absolute cost differences between different countries. Table 2.4 was used to support this statement empirically by shading those industries in which the net trade flow was in accordance with the absolute cost theory. Although this is a nice way to illustrate the validity of the theory, it is hard to imagine serious researchers spending their whole day colouring tables. In the 'question 2-6' Excel file on the website the data of Table 2.4 is repeated. Try to find a suitable way to illustrate the absolute cost theory graphically. What do you conclude from your graph?

Question 2.7

Adam Smith's classic *An Inquiry into the Nature and Causes of the Wealth of Nations* is not only available in the university or college library but also on the internet. It begins (Book I, Chapter 1) with the famous 'pin-factory' example. To what economic principle does this example refer? How is this principle linked to absolute cost advantages and international trade?

3

Comparative Advantage

To determine a country's strong sectors based on technology differences only relative (or comparative) costs are important. Comparative costs are also vital for determining the terms of trade. International trade leads to welfare gains irrespective of absolute costs. The per capita welfare level, however, depends on absolute cost differences, which also explains the large international differences in wage levels.

Review questions

Question 3.1 *

The table below shows the number of labour units needed to produce one piece of garment and one game computer in China and Japan.

	Garment	Game computer
China	1	5
Japan	1/2	2

A. Which country has an absolute advantage in the production of garments and which country in the production of game computers? Explain.

B. Which country has a comparative advantage in the production of garments and which country in the production of game computers? Explain.

C. If China produces one game computer more and Japan one game computer less, how does the total garment production of China and Japan change?

D. What happens to the total garment production if Japan produces one game computer more and China one game computer less? Do your answers to question 3.1C and 3.1D show that a country should specialize its production in the sector in which it has a comparative advantage?

Question 3.2

The table below gives the amount of labour needed to produce one ship, one bicycle, and one aeroplane in Europe and Kenya within the Ricardian model.

	Ship	Bicycle	Aeroplane
Kenya	200	50	500
Europe	100	30	200

A. Which country has an absolute advantage in the production of ships, bicycles, and planes?

B. What is Europe's comparative advantage if we only look at ships and bicycles?

C. What is Europe's comparative advantage if we only look at bicycles and aeroplanes?

D. Can you infer from your calculations in 3.2B and 3.2C which product Europe will export for sure and which product it surely will not export? Why?

E. Which product will Kenya produce for sure and which one not? Why?

Question 3.3*

Go back to the example of question 3.1 in which Japan could produce garments and game computers. Remember that producing one piece of garment in Japan required 1/2 unit of labour and producing a game computer required 4 units of labour. Furthermore, it is given that Japan is endowed with 200 units of labour.

A. Draw the production possibility frontier of Japan.

B. What are the consumption possibilities if Japan is in autarky?

Suppose that the world market price for game computers is 4.5 pieces of garment.

C. What are the consumption possibilities if Japan is trading with the rest of the world?

D. Why does Japan gain from production specialization and trade?

Question 3.4

Assume that there are two countries, Europe and Kenya, producing two goods, cars and textiles. There are 200 labourers available in Europe and 120 labourers in Kenya. The figure gives the production possibility frontiers for both Europe and Kenya.

A. What is the state of technology in both countries (the number of units of labour needed to produce textiles and cars both in Europe and Kenya)?

Assume that the consumers in both countries want to consume at least some units of both goods.

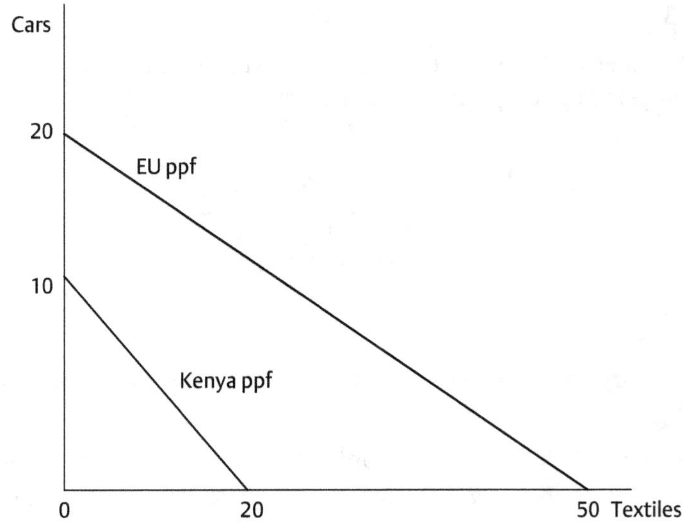

B. What is the equilibrium price of a car (expressed in units of textiles) in a situation of autarky in Europe? What will this price be in Kenya?

C. Which products will Kenya and Europe export according to the theory of comparative advantage?

D. Which price range (expressed as the price of a car in units of textiles) will make trade between Europe and Kenya possible?

E. Which price range (expressed as the price of a car in units of textiles) makes specialization of production in both countries possible?

Question 3.5

So far you have been confronted with linear production possibility frontiers. This linearity is the consequence of the double assumption of constant returns to scale and one factor of production. What will the production possibility frontier look like if there are decreasing returns to scale? Draw such a production possibility frontier.

Question 3.6

Assume that countries from Middle America only produce coffee and bananas. The table gives the total units of labour available in five countries, as well as the number of labour units needed to produce a kilo of coffee or a kilo of bananas.

A. Draw the total production possibility frontier of these five countries (analogous to the world production possibility frontier in section 3.7).

B. What is the connection between the production possibility frontier derived in question 3.6A and the production possibility frontier under decreasing returns to scale drawn in question 3.5?

	Total labour endowment	Labour requirements	
		Coffee	Bananas
Costa Rica	40	2	$\frac{1}{4}$
E1 Salvador	60	$2\frac{1}{2}$	1
Guatemala	110	4	$1\frac{1}{4}$
Honduras	60	2	$\frac{3}{4}$
Nicaragua	50	$2\frac{1}{2}$	$\frac{1}{2}$

Question 3.7

In Figure 2.2 of Chapter 2 it is argued that the observations on food and cars are in accordance with absolute cost advantage, while in Figure 3.5 it is argued that the observations on food and chemicals are in accordance with comparative advantage. In Figure 2.2, however, food is in the upper left corner of the diagram, while in Figure 3.5 food is in the upper right corner. Explain why the conclusions drawn in the text are correct despite this difference.

Empirical questions

Question 3.8

The following is taken from an American internet site:

> During the industrial revolution, a period where our nation experienced the greatest economic boom in its history, the United States utilized protectionist tariffs, and wages were steadily on the rise. In the 1970's, our companies began to move offshore, and the government went along with a massive deregulation of imports so these companies could get their products in because they were moving out. Also in the 1970's, wages began a steady decline as companies took advantage of cheap labour abroad to satisfy the consumer's supposed desire for cheaper prices, and that wage decline continues today. Is there a connection between companies shutting down domestic production, laying off Americans, employing cheap labour to ship products back to the United States and the decline of the American standard of living? You bet there is![1]

Discuss this quote based on the knowledge you obtained from studying Chapter 3.

Question 3.9

Try to find Krugman's article 'Ricardo's difficult idea' on the internet (a paper for a free trade conference in Manchester in 1996). It not only explains why major

1 *Source*: http://www.buyamerican.cc/protectionism.shtml, 2001.

intellectuals don't seem to understand comparative advantage, but also gives some recommendations for economists who want to reach a wider audience.

A. Why do only a few people understand Ricardo's idea of comparative advantage?

B. Which implicit assumptions underlie the basic Ricardian model?

Question 3.10

Many politicians and intellectuals do not seem to understand the idea of comparative advantage. Search the internet for examples (just try the search terms 'Ricardo' and 'comparative advantage'). Why do some people fail to understand Ricardo's idea?

Question 3.11

In section 3.6 the theory of comparative advantage was empirically analyzed for Europe and Kenya. First by calculating the Kenyan 'export(%)–import(%)' indicator:

$$\text{export(\%)–import(\%)} = \frac{\text{Export industry } i}{\text{Total exports}} - \frac{\text{Import industry } i}{\text{Total imports}}$$

Second, by calculating the relative productivity ratio:

$$\text{Relative productivity ratio} = \frac{\left(\dfrac{\text{productivity Kenya industry } i}{\text{productivity Europe industry } i}\right)}{\left(\dfrac{\text{productivity Kenya manufacturing sector}}{\text{productivity Europe manufacturing sector}}\right)}$$

Industry *i* was classified to trade according to comparative advantage if the first indicator was positive and the second indicator above one, or if the first indicator was negative and the second indicator below one.

The 'question 3-11' Excel file on the website contains data for exports, imports, and productivity for Japan and the Philippines, rather than Kenya and Europe. If you repeat the analysis of section 3.6 for these two countries, which sectors behave in accordance with comparative advantage? How well does comparative advantage explain the international trade flows between Japan and the Philippines? Explain.

Simulation questions

Question 3.12

The 'question 3-12' Excel file on the website allows you to experiment with the situation described in Figure 3.3 of the book, which shows the production possibility frontier and budget lines of the EU and Kenya for food and chemicals. The simulation allows you to modify the figure by changing the labour endowments, the labour requirements, or the terms of trade. We assume that Kenya and the EU are the only two countries in the world, and that consumers in both countries want to consume both goods.

The simulation has the starting values: $a_F^{EU} = 2$, $a_C^{EU} = 8$, $a_F^K = 4$, $a_C^k = 24$, labour endowment EU = 200, labour endowment Kenya = 120, and terms of trade = 0. Note that some of the values have to be changed before you can answer the questions below.

A. How many units of food and how many units of chemicals do Kenya and the EU produce if the terms of trade is one unit of food per unit of chemicals? What if the terms of trade is two units of food per unit of chemicals? Continue to answer this question until you have reached a terms of trade of ten units of food per unit of chemicals. Fill in your answers in the table below.

Terms of trade	1	2	3	4	5	6	7	8	9	10
Food production										
Chemical production										

B. Determine the range within which the terms of trade may vary in order for an equilibrium situation to arise. Explain.

C. Does this range change if you change the labour endowments?

D. Does this range change if you change the labour requirements?

Technical questions

Question 3.13

In Figure 3.3 the equilibrium terms of trade is assumed to be 4.8 units of food per unit of chemicals, which is higher than the autarky equilibrium price of 4 for the EU. The EU will therefore produce only chemicals. In Box 2.1 it is argued that in a constant returns to scale production structure firms want to produce an infinite amount if the price exceeds the cost of production. This is a situation which cannot be an economy-wide equilibrium in view of the finite amount of resources available. Given that the international trade price is higher than the autarky price for the EU, why is it possible for Figure 3.3 to be an equilibrium? That is, shouldn't the producers of the EU supply an infinite amount of chemicals according to Box 2.1?

Part II

Neoclassical Trade

4

Production Structure

The neoclassical driving forces behind international trade flows are differences in factor endowments between nations. The conclusions depend to a large extent on the production structure of the economy, based on identical technology, constant returns to scale, and perfect competition. Chapter 4 briefly reviews the microeconomic foundations and main implications of this production structure.

Review questions

Question 4.1

State the key differences in assumptions underlying the Ricardian model of international trade and the neoclassical model of international trade.

Question 4.2*

Chapter 4 uses a Cobb–Douglas production function for manufactures and food:

$$M = K_m^{\alpha_m} L_m^{1-\alpha_m}, \qquad F = K_f^{\alpha_f} L_f^{1-\alpha_f}$$

where M is the amount of manufactures produced, K_m is the amount of capital used for the production of manufactures, L_m is the amount of labour used for the production of manufactures, and α_m is a parameter between 0 and 1. Similarly for food with sub-index f.

A. The Cobb–Douglas production functions above exhibit constant returns to scale (CRS). Which aspect of the exponents in the functions ensures CRS?

B. Give a numerical example in which you show that for $\alpha_m = 0.2$ and some arbitrary choice of capital and labour inputs, the production function for manufactures above exhibits CRS.

C. Starting from any arbitrary input mix, decreasing the labour input requires additional capital to keep the production level constant. Is this additional capital requirement larger if $\alpha_m = 0.2$ or if $\alpha_m = 0.5$? What is the economic intuition behind this observation?

It is assumed throughout the book that the production of manufactures is more capital intensive than the production of food.

D. Given this assumption, what do we know now about the parameters α_m and α_f? Draw in one graph the isoquants for the production of one unit of manufactures and one unit of food.

Question 4.3

A. An isoquant depicts the set of all *efficient* input combinations. What do we mean by *efficient*?

B. Given the isoquant depicted in Figure 4.2, what can we say about all the input combinations above the isoquant? What can we say about the input combinations below the isoquant?

C. The graph displays four isoquants, including an isoquant for $M = 1$. Which isoquant for $M = 2$ corresponds to constant returns to scale relative to the given $M = 1$ isoquant?

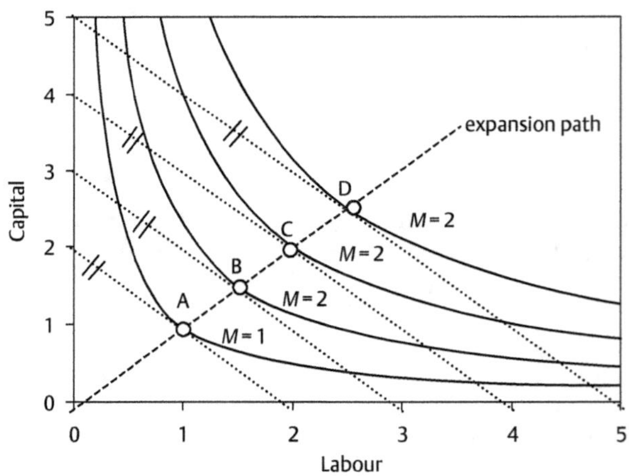

D. What can you say about points that lie on and off the expansion path?

E. Figure 4.3 shows the isoquant for $M = 1$ if α_m varies. What do you think the isoquant looks like if α_m is very close to zero? And for α_m almost equal to one? What does the parameter α_m represent in the neoclassical model?

Question 4.4

An entrepreneur produces computers using high-skilled labourers (H) and low-skilled labourers (L), with the following production function: $C = H_c^{0.6} L_c^{0.4}$. To maximize profits, the entrepreneur needs to determine the optimal (cost minimizing) ratio of high- to low-skilled labourers for each output level of computers. She knows that this is the same ratio, regardless of the output level, because of the constant returns to scale production function. It therefore suffices to determine the cost minimizing input combination for the production of one computer. The entrepreneur draws some graphs to assist her in the cost minimizing decision making process.

A. Draw the production isoquant for $C = 1$ (calculate some points and draw a smooth line through them).

The low-skill labourers receive a wage rate equal to w_L and the high-skill workers are given a wage rate equal to w_H.

B. The computer firm faces wage rates of $w_L = 1$ and $w_H = 2$. Draw some isocost lines, including the optimal one for $C = 1$.

The entrepreneur now knows (graphically) the optimal ratio of high-skilled labour to low-skilled labour. However, since she is a price taker on the labour markets, she must adjust the optimal input mix if the wage rates change.

C. Suppose the wage rate for high-skilled workers falls to $w_H = 1.5$. Draw a new graph with the new and old isocost line, and determine the new optimal input combination for high-skilled labour to low-skilled labour. What is the economic intuition for the observed substitution of the two labour inputs?

D. How does the entrepreneur determine the optimal output level, once she has decided (using the procedure above) upon the optimal (cost minimizing) input mix, that is how does she determine how many labourers to hire of each type?

Question 4.5

A. What are the two main exogenous forces determining the optimal capital–labour ratio for the producers of food and manufactures in the neoclassical model?

B. Suppose all countries in the world produce only food and manufactures, using the same technology, in a neoclassical model without international trade. What do you think will be the pattern of wage–rental ratios in the food sector of the countries in Table 4.2? How about the manufacturing sector?

Empirical questions

Question 4.6

In the 'question 4-6' Excel file on the website you can find the capital stock, labour force, and GDP per worker for a large number of countries.

A. Is there a relationship between GDP per worker and the capital stock per worker? Make a graph to illustrate your findings.

B. Can you explain this relationship?

C. Do you see this relationship reflected in tables such as Table 3.3?

D. What seems to be a crucial component for the level of economic development?

Simulation questions

Question 4.7

Consider a Dutch manufacturer who employs capital and labour in a neoclassical world to produce bicycles under constant returns to scale. The 'question 4-7' Excel file on the website is designed to assist you in determining the cost minimizing input combination of capital and labour to produce one bicycle. The file allows you to change the isocost line by changing the wage rate, rental rate, and total cost; the isoquant by changing capital intensity and production; and the point of production by changing the capital and labour input. The starting values are: $r = 1$, $w = 1$, total cost $= 2$, $\alpha = 0.5$, $X = 1$, $K = 1$, and $L = 1$. Note that some of the values have to be changed before you can answer the questions below.

As a result of the booming Dutch economy, the manager of the firm is confronted with a rising wage rate for his workers, who now receive a wage rate of 2 instead of 1. The increased wage rate forces him to reconsider the current production plan.

A. Change the simulation parameters in the file in accordance with the information above to arrive at a new cost minimizing equilibrium for the production of *one* bicycle. How many units of capital and labour does the entrepreneur use? (Hint: you can either use equation 4.A5 in the Technical Notes, or trial and error to arrive at the correct combination; your answer does not have to be exact.)

Now that she knows the optimal capital and labour inputs for the production of one bicycle the entrepreneur wants to determine what is needed to produce two bicycles.

B. Find the cost minimizing input combination for the production of two bicycles in the simulation. Is the capital–labour ratio the same as in question 4.7A? Why?

The entrepreneur is not amused by the new market conditions. She decides to change the type of bicycles she produces to become less dependent on fluctuations in labour costs.

C. Change the simulation parameter values so that we have a more capital intensive production process.

D. Find the new optimal capital–labour ratio. Did the capital–labour ratio change relative to your answer in question 4.7B? Why?

E. Did the change you made in question 4.7C affect the cost share of labour? Explain.

Technical questions

Question 4.8*

Technical Note 4.1 solves the unit cost minimization problem for a Cobb–Douglas production function. This functional form is easy to work with and gives simple solutions. There are, however, many other possible production functions. Consider, for example, the following Constant Elasticity of Substitution (CES) production function for food:

$$F = (\alpha_f K_f^{-\rho} + (1 - \alpha_f) L_f^{-\rho})^{-1/\rho}$$

A. Show that this production function also exhibits constant returns to scale by using the same procedure as in equation 4.4 of the book.

B. Define the Langrangean, as in Technical Note 4.1, and derive the first order conditions for unit cost minimization using the CES production function above.

C. Using your answer to 4.8B, determine the optimal capital–labour ratio for the firm.

D. Show that the optimal choice of labourers and capital for the production of one unit of food is:

$$K = \left(\frac{\alpha_f}{r}\right)^{1/(\rho+1)} \left[\alpha_f^{1/(\rho+1)} r^{\rho/(\rho+1)} + (1 - \alpha_f)^{1/(\rho+1)} w^{\rho/(\rho+1)}\right]^{1/\rho}$$

$$L = \left(\frac{1 - \alpha_f}{w}\right)^{1/(\rho+1)} \left[\alpha_f^{1/(\rho+1)} r^{\rho/(\rho+1)} + (1 - \alpha_f)^{1/(\rho+1)} w^{\rho/(\rho+1)}\right]^{1/\rho}$$

E. What is the minimum cost of producing one unit of food?

Question 4.9

Calculate the slope of the isoquant of food, using the CES production function given in the previous exercise. Probably the 'implicit function rule' comes in handy when making this exercise. The implicit function rule states that if you have a certain function '$F(x, y)$ = constant' and you want to take the first order derivative of y with respect to x, you can calculate:

$$\frac{dy}{dx} = -\frac{\partial F/\partial x}{\partial F/\partial y}$$

5

Factor Prices

Chapter 5 discusses the connections between the prices of final goods and the rewards to factors of production. In particular, how trade between countries can lead to factor price equalization and how an increase in the price of a final good increases the reward to the factor of production used intensively in the manufacturing process of that good.

Review questions

Question 5.1*

Two important sectors in the Australian economy are the mining sector (coal) and the agricultural sector (wool). Assume that these are the only two sectors in Australia, and that there are only two factors of production: high-skilled workers and low-skilled workers. The mining sector is high-skilled worker intensive (engineers) relative to the agricultural sector.

A. Draw the unit value isoquants for coal and wool in one figure.

B. Draw the unit value cost line in the same figure under the assumption that both goods are produced in equilibrium. Also indicate the points of production.

C. How can we derive the ratio of high-skilled to low-skilled workers for both sectors from this figure? Are your observations in line with the assumption that the mining sector is high-skilled worker intensive?

In questions 5.1A–C you have developed all the tools necessary to derive the factor price equalization proposition.

D. State the factor price equalization proposition as precisely as possible.

E. Suppose we know the prices of the final goods (coal and wool). How can we derive the factor prices (the wage rates for high-skilled and low-skilled workers)?

Question 5.2*

Consider again the Australian example of question 5.1. Initially, the final goods prices are p_{coal_0} and p_{wool_0}, and the factor prices w_{high_0} and w_{low_0}. However, at a certain moment in time the coal market collapses and the price for coal decreases.

A. The initial situation is represented by the graph of question 5.1B. Draw a new graph with the unit value isoquants for coal and wool, and a unit value cost line representing the changes resulting from the price decrease for coal.

B. What happens to the wage rates of the high-skilled and low-skilled workers? Explain.

C. Assume that both high-skilled and low-skilled workers purchased 1 ton of coal and 1 ton of wool per person before the price decrease for coal. If both types of workers buy 1 ton of wool after the price change, are they still able to buy 1 ton of coal?

D. Assume again that both high- and low-skilled workers purchased 1 ton of coal and 1 ton of wool per person before the price decrease for coal. If both types of workers still buy 1 ton of coal after the price change, are they still able to buy 1 ton of wool?

Question 5.3

The Russians and the Germans both like vodka and beer. Suppose that these are the only two products they consume and produce. Moreover, suppose that as a result of regulations vodka and beer cannot be traded between Russia and Germany initially.

Beer is produced with the help of machines largely controlled by computers. Beer breweries are therefore capital intensive. The production process of vodka, on the other hand, is more traditional and therefore quite labour intensive.

Because of its large population and lack of capital goods, the wage–rental ratio (w/r) is initially lower in Russia than in Germany.

A. In the initial situation, in which the two countries cannot trade, will the price ratio of vodka against beer (P_{vodka}/P_{beer}) be higher in Russia or in Germany?

Suppose that, after intensive international consultations, the regulations for vodka and beer are lifted. These goods can now be freely and costlessly exported and imported. In response, Russia starts to produce more vodka and less beer while Germany starts to produce more beer and less vodka. Russia exports vodka in exchange for beer.

B. Once the two countries can trade, will the price ratio of vodka against beer (P_{vodka}/P_{beer}) be higher in Russia or in Germany?

C. What will happen to the wage–rental ratio in Russia? Why?

D. What will happen to the wage–rental ratio in Holland? Why?

Question 5.4

We ask you to clarify the situation of question 5.3 graphically. The figure for question 5.4 depicts the unit value isoquant for beer, assumed to be equal for Russia and Germany (numéraire). You must add unit value cost lines and unit value isoquants.

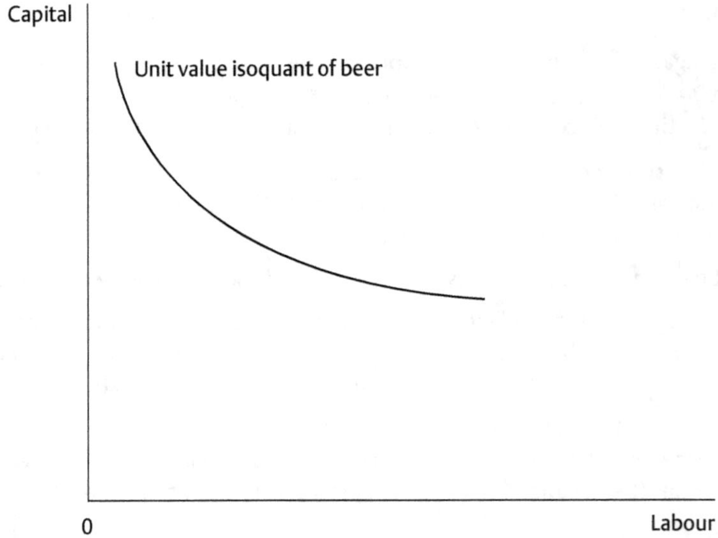

A. Draw the unit value cost lines and unit value isoquants for vodka for both Russia and Germany in a situation of autarky in the figure above.

B. What will happen to the price of beer in Russia and Germany if both countries start to trade?

C. What will happen to the price of vodka in Russia and Germany if both countries start to trade?

D. Draw the new unit value isoquants and unit value cost lines in the figure above in a situation in which Russia and Germany engage in international trade.

E. What happens to the wage rates and rental rates in both countries?

The trade liberalizations in Russia and Germany have not remained unchallenged.

F. Which groups of people are likely to protest against the liberalizations? Why?

G. What can the politicians in Russia and Germany do in response to these protests?

Question 5.5

The factor price equalization corollary in Chapter 5 argues that international trade between countries will equalize factor prices provided that

- Both final goods are produced in both nations.
- The state of technology in the two nations is the same.

In Questions 5.3 and 5.4 Russia and Germany produced vodka and beer with the same technology. What happens if we change these assumptions?

A. Assume, for example, that Germany produces only beer and Russia both beer and vodka. Draw the new unit value isoquants and unit value cost lines. Will factor prices be equal in Russia and Germany as a result of trade? Explain.

B. Go back to the situation in which both countries produce both goods. Now suppose that beer production is more capital intensive in Germany than in Russia. Draw the new unit value isoquants and unit value cost lines into the figure. Will factor prices be equal in Russia and Germany as a result of trade? Explain.

Question 5.6

In Chapter 3 we used a budget line to illustrate comparative advantage. What is the most important difference between a budget line and the unit value cost line?

Question 5.7

The Jones Magnification Effect argues that wages will fall if the price of the labour intensive good falls. This is only true if the wage rate can adapt freely. In many countries labour unions and/or labour contracts prevent wages from (quickly) falling. What do you think happens if the price of the labour intensive good falls and the wage rate cannot adapt downwards?

Empirical questions

Question 5.8

If the price equalization proposition holds, one would expect that wage rates move in unison or at least have a tendency to converge for countries that trade intensively with each other. Let's see if this is true for Canada and the United States. Search the internet for wage data. Use these data in a graph to illustrate if the factor price equalization proposition holds.

Wage data for Canada and the USA are available at the following websites:

- The International Labour Organization (http://www.ilo.org/), a specialized UN agency. See for example the 'LABORSTA' database.
- The Bureau of Labour Statistics (http://stats.bls.gov/) for the USA.
- Statistics Canada (http://www.statcan.ca/) for Canada.

Question 5.9

According to the factor price equalization proposition, wages in different countries should converge as a result of international trade. This should, for example, hold for the countries in the European Union (EU), which have formed a common economic market. The 'question 5-9' Excel file on the website contains wage rate and employment data for thirteen members of the EU. Use these data to see if the wage rates in the EU countries converge or not.

Question 5.10

The World Bank is an international organization (established in 1944) with the main task of improving the structural conditions for long-run growth in (especially) the developing countries. On its website (http://www.worldbank.org/) the World Bank offers economic data and publications. Moreover, the articles published in the *World Bank Economic Review (WBER)* are downloadable. Try to find the article 'Why has Poland avoided the price liberalization trap? The case of the hog-pork sector' written by A. Wei, W. Guba, and R. Burcroff.

If you read the Stolper–Samuelson proposition it looks as if the necessary adjustments of factor prices in response to changes in commodity prices is an easy process. The article by Wei *et al.* shows that this is far from the truth. What is the 'price liberalization trap' and why does it appear? How could the Polish hog-pork sector avoid the trap?

Simulation questions

Question 5.11

The simulation in the 'question 5-11' Excel file on the website repeats the Lerner diagram drawn in Figure 5.4. We have assumed initially that capital's share for manufactures is 80 per cent and for food is 20 per cent ($\alpha_m = 0.8$ and $\alpha_f = 0.2$). Furthermore, the wage rate w and rental rate r are equal to $w = r = 0.2$. The simulation allows you to change the wage rate and the rental rate.

A. What is the capital intensive and what the labour intensive good in the simulation? Explain in two different ways.

B. The Lerner diagram pictures the unit value isoquants of manufactures and food. Why is the production of manufactures and food not equal to unity?

C. If you increase the wage rate, what happens to the prices of manufactures and food? What happens to the labour input and capital input? Explain.

D. Fill in the table below by changing the wage rate in the simulation while keeping the rental rate equal to 0.2. Comment on the evolution of the *final goods prices*.

Wage rate	0.1	0.2	0.3	0.4	0.5	0.6	0.7	0.8	0.9
Price manufactures									
Price food									

E. Similarly, fill in the table below by changing the wage rate in the simulation while keeping the rental rate at 0.2. Comment on the evolution of the *factor inputs*.

Wage rate	0.1	0.2	0.3	0.4	0.5	0.6	0.7	0.8	0.9
Labour input manufactures									
Capital input manufactures									

Question 5.12

We will again analyse the Lerner diagram. Instead of deriving final goods prices from factor prices, the simulation in the 'question 5-12' Excel file on the website derives factor prices from final goods prices, as in the Stolper–Samuelson proposition. Initially, we assume $\alpha_m = 0.8$, $\alpha_f = 0.2$, $p_m = 0.3$, and $p_f = 0.3$.

A. Increase the price of manufactures in the simulation. What happens to the wage rate and rental rate? What happens to the factor inputs? Explain.

B. Fill in the table below by changing the price of manufactures while keeping the price of food stable at 0.3. Comment on the development of the *factor prices*.

Price manufactures	0.1	0.2	0.3	0.4	0.5	0.6	0.7	0.8	0.9
Wage rate									
Rental rate									

C. Also, fill in the table below by changing the price of manufactures while keeping the price of food stable at 0.3. Comment on the development of the *factor inputs*.

Price manufactures	0.1	0.2	0.3	0.4	0.5	0.6	0.7	0.8	0.9
Labour input manufactures									
Capital manufactures									

Question 5.13

Prices are not the only exogenous variables in the model of Chapter 5. The factor intensities (alpha) are also given. This question analyses the impact of changing the factor intensities for factor prices and final goods prices using both simulations 'question 5-11' and 'question 5-12' on the website.

A. Fill in the table below while assuming that final goods prices remain constant, given that $\alpha_m = 0.8$. Comment on the development of the *factor prices*.

Alpha food	0.1	0.2	0.3	0.4	0.5	0.6	0.7	0.8	0.9
Wage rate									
Rental rate									

B. Fill in the table below while assuming that factor prices remain constant, given that $\alpha_m = 0.8$. Comment on the development of the final *goods prices*.

Alpha food	0.1	0.2	0.3	0.4	0.5	0.6	0.7	0.8	0.9
Price manufactures									
Price food									

Technical questions

Question 5.14

Equation (5.A6) in technical note 5.2 gives the relationship between relative changes in final goods prices and factor prices. These equations can easily be modified for the situation described by question 5.1, where we assumed that Australia has only two sectors of production: the high-skilled intensive mining sector producing coal and the low-skilled intensive agricultural sector producing wool. Let α be the high-skilled labour intensity parameter for the production of coal and β the high-skilled labour intensity parameter for the production of wool. The equations then become:

$$\tilde{w}_{low} = \frac{\alpha}{\alpha - \beta}\tilde{p}_{wool} - \frac{\beta}{\alpha - \beta}\tilde{p}_{coal}$$

$$\tilde{w}_{high} = \frac{1-\beta}{\alpha - \beta}\tilde{p}_{coal} - \frac{1-\alpha}{\alpha - \beta}\tilde{p}_{wool}$$

Show with the help of these two equations that a decrease in the price of coal leads to the conclusion that $\tilde{w}_{low} > \tilde{p}_{wool} > \tilde{p}_{coal} > \tilde{w}_{high}$.

Question 5.15

The technical notes of Chapter 5 derive the factor price equalization proposition and the Stolper–Samuelson proposition assuming that the supply side of the economy is characterized by a Cobb–Douglas production function. We will now derive these two propositions using a CES production function instead, see question 4.8. While answering this question, use the unit cost function for food derived in question 4.8.

A. What is the unit cost function of manufactures?

B. Express the final goods price of food and manufactures in terms of the wage rate and rental rate assuming perfect competition.

C. Express the wage rate and rental rate in terms of final goods prices assuming that the elasticity of substitution for capital and labour is equal for food and manufactures ($\rho_f = \rho_m$).

D. Show mathematically that the Stolper–Samuelson proposition holds if we use a CES production function.

Question 5.16

Use the results and assumptions of the previous question to prove that the Jones Magnification Effect also holds for a CES production function.

A. Calculate the partial first order derivatives of the rental rate with respect to the price of food and the price of manufactures using your result to question 5.15C.

B. Calculate the partial first order derivatives of the wage rate with respect to the price of food and the price of manufactures using your result to question 5.15C.

C. Express the relative change of the rental rate and wage rate (dr/r and dw/w) as a function of final goods prices (remember from your mathematics classes that the total differential of for example the rental rate is $dr = (\partial r/\partial p_f)dp_f + (\partial r/\partial p_m)dp_m$).

D. Show mathematically that the Jones Magnification Effect also holds for a CES function.

6

Production Volume

Chapter 6 analyses the connection between the production levels of final goods and the available factors of production. A rise in the available capital stock, for example, increases the production of capital intensive goods and decreases the production of labour intensive goods (Rybczynski effect).

Review questions

Question 6.1 *

Bangladesh is a developing country which ranks second in the top ten of unskilled-labour intensive manufacturing exporters (see Box 6.2). These exports consist mainly of clothing goods. Most inhabitants of Bangladesh are not active in the manufacturing sector, but are farmers producing rice. Both rice and clothes are produced with only two factor inputs, capital and labour. Like most developing countries, Bangladesh has a large labour force in relation to its capital stock. Assume that the production of rice is relatively labour intensive compared to the production of clothes.

A. Draw the situation described above in an Edgeworth box. Put the origin of rice in the south-west corner and the origin of clothes in the north-east corner. Measure labour on the horizontal axis and capital on the vertical axis. Draw the contract curve, an efficient point of production, and the isoquants of both goods through the efficient production point.

B. What indicates in the Edgeworth box the *level* of output of a good?

C. How can you determine the production levels of rice and clothes in full employment equilibrium?

A foreign multinational is impressed by the quality of the clothes produced in Bangladesh and by the low wage rate. After some discussions the multinational decides to 'just do it' and invests in Bangladesh by building a large factory, thus increasing the capital stock in Bangladesh.

D. Copy the Edgeworth box of question 6.1A. Assume that the increase in the capital stock does not affect the prices of rice and clothing and draw the new production point. What has happened to the production levels of rice and clothes? Why?

Question 6.2

The two graphs for question 6.2 depict Bangladesh, which produces capital intensive rice and labour intensive clothing. The first graph shows the unit value isoquants for both goods. The second graph is an Edgeworth box.

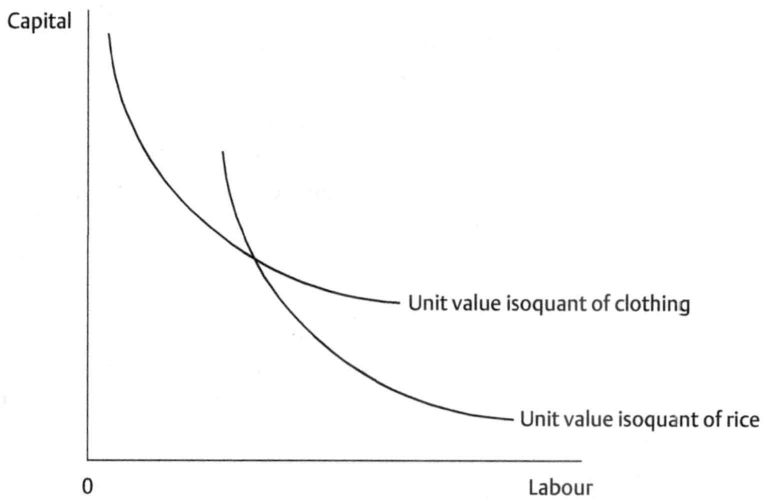

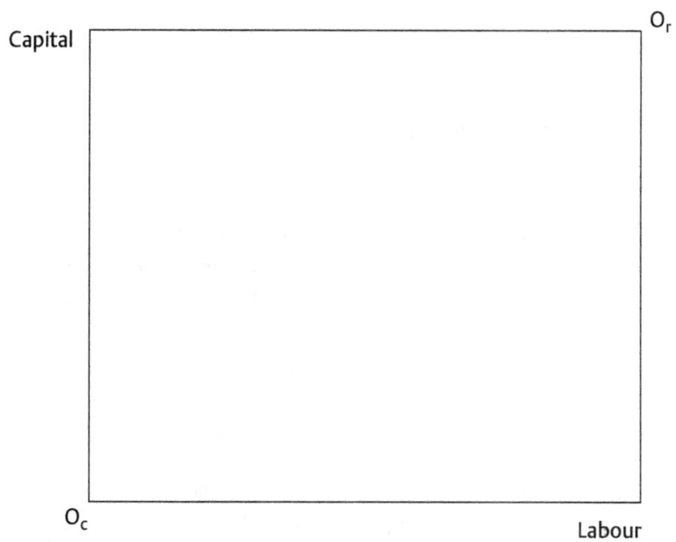

A. Draw the optimal production point in the Edgeworth box.

B. What happens if the price of clothing increases? Draw the new situation in both graphs.

C. The Rybczynski result is based on the assumption that the prices of final goods remain constant. Explain why a price rise for clothing combined with an increase in the labour stock will not necessarily lead to an increase in the production of rice.

Question 6.3

Box 6.1 describes an extension of the basic neoclassical model. Let's apply this analysis to the European Union (EU), which produces manufactures and food. The EU labour market is not as flexible as that of other countries. We assume, therefore, that the reallocation of capital is more rapid than the reallocation of labour.

A. Which production factor would you label as sector specific here?

The EU now concludes a new trade agreement with some Central and East European countries in anticipation of their eventual entry into the EU. This agreement puts extra competitive pressure on the agricultural sector in the EU, which decreases the price in that sector.

B. In a graph, draw the distribution of capital over the manufacturing sector and the agricultural sector in the EU. Illustrate the equilibrium before the price decrease, immediately after the price decrease (Ethier), and the medium-term equilibrium after the price decrease (Neary).

C. Draw the long-run equilibrium in your graph of question 6.3B. Which production factor has ultimately benefited from the price decrease? Why?

D. Who supports the removal of adjustment barriers in the labour market? Why?

Question 6.4

Chapter 4 gives the production functions for manufactures and food:

$$M = K_m^{\alpha_m} L_m^{1-\alpha_m}; \qquad F = K_f^{\alpha_f} L_f^{1-\alpha_f}; \qquad 0 < \alpha_m, \alpha_f < 1$$

Figure 6.6 depicts contract curves for different values of α_m. What will the contract curve look like if (i) $\alpha_m = \alpha_f$, (ii) $\alpha_m < \alpha_f$, or (iii) $\alpha_m > \alpha_f$? Illustrate these three contract curves in an Edgeworth box with labour on the horizontal axis and capital on the vertical axis.

Question 6.5

Imagine a country producing only CDs and pottery. The capital–labour ratio for the production of CDs is 2 and for the production of pottery is 1. The country has an initial capital endowment of 8 and labour endowment of 6. Assume throughout this exercise that all available inputs will be employed.

A. How much labour and capital will be used in the production process of CDs and how much in the production process of pottery?

At a certain moment in time, both the capital and the labour endowment increase by 2 units (so the capital endowment is now 10 and the labour endowment 8).

B. How much labour and capital will be used in the production process of CDs and how much in the production process of pottery in the new situation?

C. Compare your answers to question 6.5A and question 6.5B. Is this in accordance with the Rybczynski proposition?

Question 6.6

Section 6.6 of the book describes an empirical study of the effects of the influx of Russian immigrants into Israel, which changed the composition of the Israeli labour force. It offers an opportunity to investigate the Rybczynski proposition. When confronting theory with empirical data, you have to be careful and correct for factors that are not explicitly modelled or assumed constant in theory.

A. Which factors, not explicitly modelled or assumed constant in Chapter 6, played a role in this particular study?

B. Do you consider the simplifications a weakness of economic theory?

Empirical questions

Question 6.7

Section 6.6 shows that the immigration of Russian Jews in Israel increased the labour endowment, changed the skill composition, and affected the production structure of the Israel economy. Naturally, we can look at other case studies to try to detect the same phenomenon. In the 'question 6-7' Excel file on the website you can find immigration and population data for eight European countries. Furthermore, the value added of a number of labour intensive industries is included. Is there a positive relationship between the growth in the labour intensive industries and the growth in population due to immigration? Interpret the results of your analysis.

Question 6.8

Locate on the web or at your library the paper called 'The Rybczynski theorem, factor price-equalisation, and immigration: evidence from the United States', written by G. H. Hanson and M. J. Slaughter. As the title suggests, it is an empirical investigation of the Rybczynski theorem.

A. Why do the authors study the development of relative prices across states?

B. What effect do the authors find for the state of California?

C. Does the Rybczynski theorem help in explaining the output mix in American states?

Simulation questions

Question 6.9*

The 'question 6-9' Excel file on the website contains two figures. The first figure shows the unit value isoquants of manufactures and food. The second figure shows the Edgeworth box. Assume that we have two factors of production, workers with at least college (C), and workers with at most a highschool diploma (H). The two lines inside the Edgeworth box reflect the college educated–highschool educated ratios in the production of manufactures and food. The intersection of these two lines is the point of production. The simulation allows you to change the endowments, prices, and factor intensity parameters.

A. Show the effect of the migration of Russian Jews into Israel.

B. Suppose that Russia has the same factors of production, what does the Rybczynski proposition imply for Russian production?

The wages for high-educated workers increased somewhat in Israel due to changes in technology. There is a one-to-one relationship between wages and prices in our neoclassical framework.

C. Simulate the effect of the wage increase for college educated workers (by changing final goods prices). What happens to production levels and why? Does the Rybczynski result always hold with price changes?

D. Suppose that technological developments lead to a higher 'college-educated labour intensity' in the production of manufactures. Change the correct parameter in the simulation. What happens to the production levels? Explain.

Technical questions

Question 6.10

The CES production functions for manufactures and food are given below:

$$F = \left(\alpha_f K_f^{-\rho} + (1-\alpha_f) L_f^{-\rho}\right)^{-1/\rho}$$

$$M = \left(\alpha_m K_m^{-\rho} + (1-\alpha_m) L_m^{-\rho}\right)^{-1/\rho}$$

A. Determine the contract curve for these production functions.

B. Compute the share of labourers active in manufacturing analogous to equation (6.A4) in the technical notes.

C. Determine the production level of manufactures (analogous to equation 6.A6).

7

Factor Abundance

Chapter 7 investigates the connection between the direction of international trade flows and the factor intensity of the production process. Countries tend to export goods making intensive use of the relatively abundant factors of production (Heckscher–Ohlin result).

Review questions

Question 7.1 *

Imagine a world consisting of two countries: North Korea and South Korea. North Korea has more labourers than South Korea, but less machinery (capital).[1] Both countries produce food, a labour intensive good, and electronics, a capital intensive good. The figure for question 7.1 gives the production possibility frontier (ppf) of South Korea.

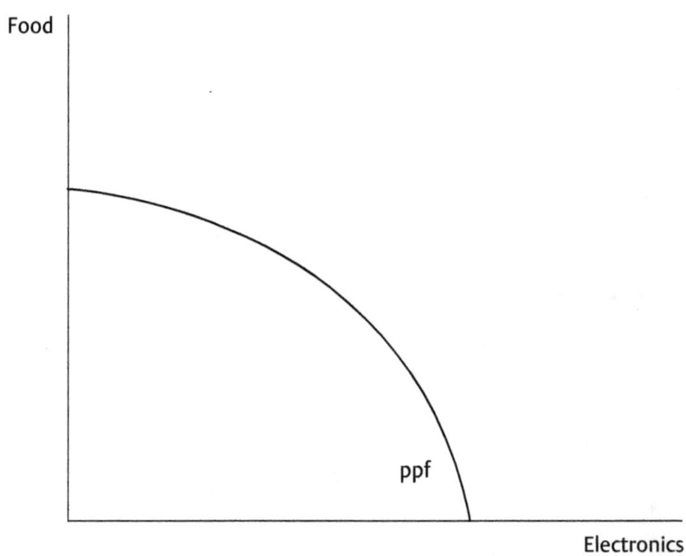

[1] This is not actually true since South Korea has more labourers than North Korea.

A. Draw the production possibility frontier of North Korea in the same figure.

B. How can we determine the production and consumption levels of food and electronics for both countries in autarky? Draw these production and consumption points in the figure above.

C. What are the autarky prices in North Korea and South Korea?

D. What happens with these prices if North Korea and South Korea start to trade with each other?

E. How can we determine the production and consumption levels of food and electronics in North Korea and South Korea if both countries are trading with each other? Draw these production and consumption points also in the figure above.

F. Which goods are imported and exported by the two countries?

G. Is this in accordance with the Heckscher–Ohlin proposition?

Question 7.2*

To derive the Heckscher–Ohlin proposition one must specify the demand side of the economy. In Chapter 7 it is based on the following utility function:

$$U = C_m^{\delta_m} C_f^{1-\delta_m}$$

A. In what respect do we have to interpret the iso-utility curves differently from the Cobb–Douglas production isoquants?

B. What is the interpretation of δ_m?

Box 7.1 discusses identical homothetic preferences (of which the above equation is an example).

C. What are identical preferences?

D. How can the introduction of heterogeneous preferences interfere with the Heckscher–Ohlin proposition?

E. What are homothetic preferences?

Section 7.3 argues that imposing identical homothetic preferences for all consumers ensures that the distribution of income over the economic agents is irrelevant for determining aggregate consumption levels since only aggregate income is important.

F. Consider a graph like Figure 7.2. Draw arbitrary, non-homothetic preferences and an income expansion path in this figure.

G. Show that the distribution of income *is* relevant for determining aggregate consumption levels in the setting of question 7.2F.

Question 7.3

Consider South Korea, a country producing capital intensive electronics and labour intensive food using capital and labour.

A. Draw the production possibility frontier of South Korea. Indicate the point of autarky production and explain why South Korea produces at this point.

B. How can you determine the autarky price in your figure?

Suppose that South Korea starts to trade with other countries. The international prices are not equal to the autarky prices in South Korea.

C. Indicate the new points of production and consumption in your figure. Be careful to make a consistent drawing.

Now suppose that South Korea is confronted with a large influx of labour through immigration, extending the South Korean labour stock.

D. Draw South Korea's new production possibility frontier.

E. What would be the new production point at constant international prices according to the Rybczynski proposition? Draw this point in the figure and explain.

F. Is this necessarily the new production point? Explain.

Question 7.4

Table 7.1 in the book shows the autarky values for Austria. The values above the double line are exogenously specified parameters. The values below the double line are determined endogenously. If we change the parameter values above the line, we should be able to determine the endogenous values below the line. Use Figure 7.10 and/or equation (7.5) to determine the changes in (i) the wage–rental rate, (ii) the final goods price ratio, (iii) the welfare level, (iv) the production level of manufactures, and (v) the production level of food if:

A. The Austrian capital stock K increases.

B. The Austrian labour force L increases.

C. The capital intensity of manufactures α_m decreases.

D. The share of income spent on manufactures δ_m increases.

Question 7.5

Assume that the world consists of two countries, A and B, which are able to trade with each other. The figure for question 7.5 depicts the initial situation using the production possibility frontiers, the income lines at international prices, and the identical homothetic preferences.

Does the situation illustrated in the figure represent an international trade equilibrium? If so, why? If not, why not and how will an international trade equilibrium be reached?

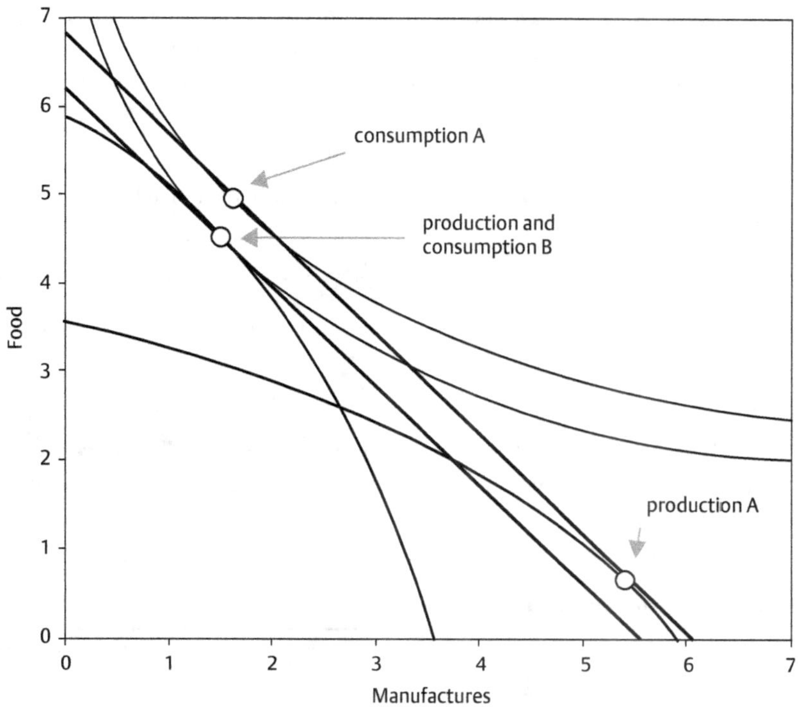

Question 7.6

Answer the following basic questions for the standard neoclassical trade model.

A. If there are no obstacles to international trade, is it possible that no trade occurs? If your answer is affirmative, under what circumstances will there be no trade?

B. Is complete specialization of production possible?

Question 7.7

Opponents of globalization often argue that free trade between the 'First' World (OECD countries) and the 'Third' World (developing countries) leads to exploitation of the Third World countries. Can you substantiate the 'exploitation' claim of these opponents based on the neoclassical model? Explain.

Empirical questions

Question 7.8

Different boxes throughout Part II (Neoclassical Trade) summarized the type of products exported by different countries. The question arises if these export patterns are in accordance with the Heckscher–Ohlin proposition. The 'question 7-8' Excel file on the website contains export data of the International Trade Centre which allows you to address this question in combination with data from the World Bank.

A. What does the Heckscher–Ohlin proposition predict?

B. Try to get a rough indication if the Heckscher–Ohlin proposition holds empirically using the data in the Excel file.

C. What criticism can you give on your own analysis?

Question 7.9

The table shows the share of skilled and unskilled workers employed in sectors exporting to the South (developing countries) and competing with imports from the South.

Skill intensity of North–South trade, 1985 (%)

	Exports to the South	Imports from the South	Export /imports
Germany			
Non-manual plus skilled manual	63.3	44.4	1.43
Semi- and unskilled manual	36.7	55.6	0.66
France			
Non-manual plus skilled manual	68.6	54.5	1.26
Semi- and unskilled manual	31.4	45.5	0.69
Italy			
Non-manual plus skilled manual	53.3	45.7	1.17
Semi- and unskilled manual	46.7	54.3	0.86
Netherlands			
Non-manual plus skilled manual	57.3	42.4	1.35
Semi- and unskilled manual	42.6	57.6	0.74
Belgium			
Non-manual plus skilled manual	57.1	47.0	1.21
Semi- and unskilled manual	42.9	53.0	0.81
United Kingdom			
Non-manual plus skilled manual	58.7	48.4	1.21
Semi- and unskilled manual	41.3	51.6	0.80

Source: D. Schumacher, 'Employment Impact in the European Community Countries of East-West Trade Flows,' International Employment Policies Working Paper 24, ILO, 1989, as reported by A. Wood, 'Give Heckscher and Ohlin a Chance!,' Weltwirtschaftliches Archiv, 1994.

Based on the numbers in the table, discuss if the Heckscher–Ohlin proposition holds empirically.

Simulation questions

Question 7.10

The 'question 7-10' Excel file on the website displays an autarky equilibrium for the economy of North Korea, producing only food (f) and rockets (r). Arguably, the North Korean economy comes closest to the theoretical situation of complete autarky. The simulation automatically adjusts all three curves to display the equilibrium point. The initial parameters for the simulation are: $\alpha_f = 0.3$; $\alpha_r = 0.7$; $K = 2$; $L = 5$; $\delta_f = 0.4$.

The government of North Korea starts a new policy to promote building rockets to threaten Japan and the United States. As a result of this policy the share of capital in the production process for rockets increases by ten percentage points. Unfortunately, a slight policy oversight caused the government to neglect food production, leading to widespread famine in North Korea (remember that importing food is impossible). As a secondary result of the policy, therefore the labour force decreases by 40 per cent.

A. Simulate the effects of the North Korean policy.

B. How do prices, income, utility, and production of the North Korean economy change? Explain why these changes occur.

The leaders of North Korea manage to extract concessions from the United States. In return for the promise not to fire any more rockets North Korea receives two nuclear power plants. This significantly increases the capital stock of the country, namely by 50 per cent. The Chinese government is concerned about the growing influence of America in North Korea. To support the North Korean regime the Chinese decide to deport all the North Korean refugees who where seeking shelter in China back to their motherland. Consequently, the North Korean labour force now grows by 33.3 per cent.

C. Simulate these new developments.

D. How do prices, income, utility, and production of the North Korean economy change? Explain.

In response to all this good news the North Korean government secretly decides to increase spending on its pet project. The share of income spent on rockets doubles.

E. After the implementation of this policy total income decreases but welfare (= total utility) increases. Can you explain why?

F. Naturally, the North Korean population is not too happy with this last policy change. Explain why we do not see this reflected in our model of the economy.

Question 7.11

The government of North Korea (see question 7.10) decides that it needs at least one friend in this world to trade with. As they are aware of the implications of the neoclassical trade model they decide to trade only with countries with the same homothetic preferences and production technology. After searching the globe they decide to trade with Libya, characterized by the following economic parameters:

$$\alpha_f = 0.7; \alpha_r = 0.3; K = 1; L = 2; \delta_f = 0.4$$

As a result of international restrictions Libya and North Korea do not trade with other countries in the world. The North Korean economy is characterized by the following parameters: $\alpha_f = 0.3$; $\alpha_r = 0.7$; $K = 3$; $L = 4$; $\delta_f = 0.4$.

A. Simulate the autarky situation of both economies using the 'question 7-11' Excel file on the website. Which country produces relatively more rockets?

B. At which prices will trade between North Korea and Libya be possible?

Assume that Libya and North Korea start to trade with each other.

C. Which good will North Korea export, and which good will it import? Why?

The North Korean government has doubts about the validity of the assumptions of the neoclassical model. In particular, it is not sure if Libya has the same preferences as North Korea.

D. Will Libya export the same good for every value of δ_f? Explain.

E. Is complete specialization of production possible in the neoclassical model? Show this with the assistance of your simulation.

Technical questions

Question 7.12

In addition to CES production functions we can also use a CES utility function, which can be written as:

$$U = \left(\delta_m C_m^{-\mu} + (1 - \delta_m) C_f^{-\mu}\right)^{-1/\mu}$$

A. What is the budget constraint facing a consumer?

B. Define the Langrangean for the problem of the consumer (maximize utility, given the budget constraint). Derive the first order conditions for utility maximization using the CES function above.

C. Determine the optimal consumption ratio of manufactures and food, given final good prices.

D. What is the demand function for manufactures?

8

Trade Policy

Chapter 8 analyses the impact of trade policy on the size of trade flows, focusing in particular on the distribution of winners (protected domestic producers) and losers (consumers, the country as a whole, and other countries). The welfare distribution aspects of trade policy make the demand for protection (lobbying) understandable.

Review questions

Question 8.1

Consider the production process of cars in China, which uses steel as an intermediate input as summarized in the table.

Good	World price	Tariff (%)	Domestic price
Cars	100	20	120
Steel	60	10	66
Available for processing stage	40	35	54

The Chinese government wants to promote the local manufacturing of cars and is searching for ways to improve the competitive position of its car industry.

A. Which tariff (on car imports or steel imports) should the government increase, in order to stimulate the local production of cars in China?

The United States and Japan object to the protective tariffs on the Chinese car market, which forces their firms either to build factories in China (to circumvent the import tariff) or to lose market share relative to domestic producers. After an intense lobbying process the Chinese government reduces the tariff on cars to 17 per cent.

B. What should the Chinese government do to keep the effective rate of protection on the local production of cars constant (at 35 per cent)?

C. Is it possible for the Chinese government to impose a negative effective tariff on the local production of cars? If so, how?

Question 8.2

The European Union (EU) is considered to be a 'large' country in this question. In the 1980s Japanese producers began to export many cars to the EU. To protect their domestic car industries, the governments of the EU countries pushed for protective tariffs. We analyse the impact of these tariffs in a partial equilibrium framework.

A. What makes a partial equilibrium analysis 'partial'?

B. Draw a partial equilibrium figure of the EU car market. Indicate clearly the volume of Japanese imports before and after the imposition of the tariff.

C. Is the tariff welfare improving for the EU? Why, or why not?

The Japanese car manufacturers were not happy with the EU protection and started a lobbying process in Brussels to abolish the EU tariffs. These lobbying efforts were not completely successful, such that the tariffs are abolished in return for a 'voluntary' restriction of car exports to the EU.

D. Why do the Japanese firms prefer the voluntary export restrains (VERs) to the tariffs?

E. What is the tariff-equivalent import quota (or rather VER in this question) for Japan in your figure for question 8.2B?

Question 8.3*

A military coup in Zombio has overthrown the government. The new leaders, proud defenders of the national heritage, declare that all Western food imports will be subject to a tax of 10 per cent, to be paid at the customs office. As the leading economist in Zombio you are invited to evaluate this measure.

A. What is the correct economic term for this tariff?

Zombio produces and consumes two goods, namely copper and food. The figure for question 8.3 summarizes the free trade situation.

B. Is copper imported or exported in the free trade situation? Explain how you can derive this information from the graph.

C. Explain what happens to the production of copper and food in Zombio if the military leaders impose a tariff τ on imports. Illustrate this in the graph and label the new production point P'.

D. What are the new consumption possibilities for Zombio (at world prices) generated by the production point P'? Indicate these possibilities in your graph.

E. Let C' be the utility maximizing consumption choice of consumers, given the consumption possibilities available to them (see question 8.3D). Illustrate point C' in your graph.

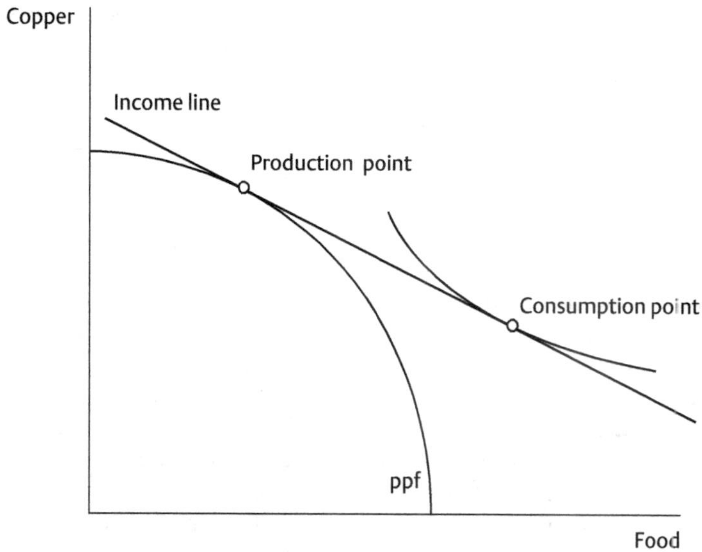

F. Why do the consumers choose a different consumption point from your answer to question 8.3E? Denote the actual consumption point from your graph with C″.

G. Explain what the two distorting effects of the tariff are, and where you have illustrated them in this question.

The offer curves analysis of Chapter 8 shows that countries might gain from imposing a tariff under specific circumstances.

H. Since Zombio is a small country it cannot influence world prices. What is the shape of the offer curve of the rest of the world?

I. What happens to Zombio's offer curve if it imposes a tariff?

Question 8.4

The government of Zombio (see question 8.3) could also decide to give a production subsidy to the food industry to protect the national food sector. You are asked to evaluate this per unit subsidy s, which increases the return per unit of output for the producers of food to $p_{food}(1 + s)$.

A. Draw the new budget constraint and the new production point after the introduction of the subsidy in a general equilibrium framework (use the graph of question 8.3 as your starting point).

We assume that *world prices are unaffected* by the subsidy (Zombio is a small country and has a negligible influence on world prices). Moreover, the government taxes the consumers to pay for the subsidy and balance the budget. Note that the consumers continue to pay world prices.

B. Draw the new budget constraint at world prices as well as the new consumption point. Assume that preferences are identical and homothetic. Does the consumption of food increase or decrease after the subsidy?

C. According to section 8.4 imposing a tariff leads to a double distortion. Is a production subsidy as distortive as a tariff?

Question 8.5

Import substitution is a development strategy based on the 'infant industry' argument, which temporarily protects a relatively young sector from foreign competition to give this sector the chance to 'grow up' and become more productive.[1] During the (short?) time period of protection the sector can, for example, educate its workforce or improve its distribution system. After a while, the sector has matured, is able to compete with the rest of the world, and the protection can stop. The process is summarized for Brazil in the figure for question 8.5.

Let AA′ be Brazil's initial production possibility frontier. The economy produces at point 1, Brazil exports *b* coffee and imports *a* cars. Assuming that the 'infant industry' argument is valid, the Brazilian economy can reach point 2 over time by imposing a temporary import tariff on cars. In the new equilibrium, the production of cars is increased and imports are lower than before.

A. Use the figure to describe how the infant industry argument works for Brazil. Also explain why it is essential that protection leads to an improvement in technology in the national car industry.

B. What are some of the potential pitfalls for a government that tries to pursue a policy of protecting 'infant' industries?

Question 8.6

The terms of trade of a country is defined as the price of its exports, divided by the price of its imports. Trade triangles show the size of exports and imports of a country.

A. What is the relationship between the terms of trade and an offer curve?

B. What is the relationship between trade triangles and offer curves?

Question 8.7*

Suppose that the European Union (EU) and the United States (USA) both produce bananas and steel, where the EU exports steel in return for American bananas.

A. Draw the offer curves of the EU and the USA in one figure. The trade of steel is measured on the horizontal axis and the trade of bananas is measured on the vertical axis. Indicate clearly which offer curve belongs to which country.

B. Illustrate the international trade equilibrium in your figure of question 8.7A, also showing the traded amounts of each product.

[1] Sometimes referred to as the infantile industry argument.

C. Show in your figure the effects of a 'trade war' on welfare and trade, assuming that, starting from free trade, one country imposes an 'optimal tariff' and the other country retaliates once. Does it matter which country starts the trade war?

Suppose now that, starting from free trade, the USA and the EU simultaneously impose 'optimal tariffs'.

D. Is the resulting outcome welfare maximizing for either country and/or for the world as a whole? What is this welfare situation called in game theory?

E. Is the above analysis relevant for the establishment and functioning of international trade organizations such as the WTO (World Trade Organization)?

Question 8.8

The tariff analysis in Chapter 8 gives us no reason to abandon the paradigm of free trade. Nonetheless, almost all countries in the world impose some type of artificial barriers to international trade flows. This is, perhaps, not only the result of a failure of economic policy makers to read and study the book and the accompanying study guide, but is also related to the nature of the economic effects of tariffs.

Consider the US steel industry, which has been going through some rough times recently. The growing competitiveness of, for example, Russian steel companies, continues to erode the market share of domestic US producers. The American government acts decisively and imposes a tariff on the Russian steel imports, in order to save the jobs of many American steelworkers.

A. Who benefits and who loses in the USA as a result of the tariff? What is the main reason, in your view, for the absence of lobbying efforts for the losers?

Consider the African country Tanzania. The government is short of cash for financing the necessary public services in its large country. Against the advice of the IMF and the World Bank, it imposes a tariff on manufactures from the European Union.

B. Why do you think the Tanzanian government budget depends to a large extent on tariff revenues?

Empirical questions

Question 8.9

Chapter 8 and earlier chapters of the book give strong theoretical support for free trade. For various reasons a country enjoys welfare improvements if it opens its borders to international trade flows. Let us see whether this welfare improvement can be substantiated empirically. The 'question 8-9' Excel file on the website contains data on the average tariff, GDP per capita, exports, and imports for sixty-three countries.

A. Which ten countries have the lowest trade tariffs?

B. Which ten countries have the highest tariffs?

C. Compare your answers to questions 8.9A and 8.9B. What is the main difference between these countries?

D. How are free trade and welfare empirically related in this sample?

E. If free trade is welfare improving for all countries, can you give some possible motives for the countries in the sample to impose high tariff rates?

Question 8.10

Chapter 8 is concerned with the theoretical analysis of trade protection, mainly focusing on tariffs. We have seen that there is a strong case for support of free trade, although many countries choose to erect barriers to international trade. The economic researchers A. M. Mayda and D. Rodrik have asked themselves an intriguing question: 'Why are some people (and countries) more protectionist than others?' This is the title of a paper to be found at your university library or on the web. Go to http://www.nber.org and download the working paper.

A. What affects the attitudes of individuals toward trade? Can we link this to our findings in the models of this and previous chapters?

B. Are there other empirically relevant reasons for protectionism that we do not take into account in our economic models?

C. Does the paper offer an explanation for the popularity of protectionism as an economic policy, in contrast to the theoretical wisdom of free trade?

Simulation questions

Question 8.11

The 'question 8-11' Excel file on the website depicts the free trade equilibrium for Zombio, which produces coffee and tractors. In the simulation you can change the tariff rate on tractors, the share of income spent on tractors, the fractor endowments, and the world price of tractors. The junta in charge wants to raise some revenue to pay the wages of its soldiers. Rather than imposing taxes on domestically produced goods, the government decides to raise import duties to 50 per cent.

The simulation has the starting values: $K = 2$, $L = 7$, Tariff $= 0$, $\delta_m = 0.5$. Note that some of the values have to be changed before you can answer the questions below.

A. Simulate the policy change of the government. Which group in Zombio is benefiting from the policy and why? What is the total income cost (in terms of tractors) of the policy for Zombio?

The world market for tractors is booming. The increased demand from other countries increases the relative price of tractors by 20 per cent.

B. What does this mean for the terms of trade for Zombio?

C. What happens to utility and income (in terms of tractors)? Why?

As a result of the high tariff rate the local tractor industry faces less competition from abroad, becomes corrupted, and through mismanagement loses half of Zombio's capital stock.

D. Simulate the decline in the capital stock. Why does the volume of trade increase?

The junta has been talking about the benefits of the revolution for such a long time that the people of Zombio become thirsty for more coffee. They start to spend a larger share of their income on coffee than before.

E. Change the correct simulation parameter to reflect the change in preferences. What happens to the volume of trade and why?

Part III

New Trade

9

Imperfect Competition

Chapter 9 analyses the impact of international trade on production, consumption, and welfare if firms are not price takers but realize that they possess market power.

Review questions

Question 9.1

Let's first review some of the concepts discussed in Chapter 9.

A. What are pro-competitive gains from trade?

B. What are iceberg transport costs?

C. Why do pro-competitive gains from trade arise if transport costs are sufficiently small, and not if transport costs are very high?

Question 9.2

Suppose the German government protects the electricity market by allowing only one firm to supply electricity. The figure for question 9.2 gives the production possibilities frontier (ppf) and two consumer iso-utility curves for Germany.

A. Which production point would be attained under perfect competition? Also indicate the price of electricity relative to housing in the figure.

B. Recall that the German electricity market is characterized by a monopoly. Indicate in the figure where the production point under monopoly could be located. Also indicate the price of electricity relative to housing under monopoly.

C. Compare the relative prices of electricity in questions 9.2A and 9.2B. How and why do they differ?

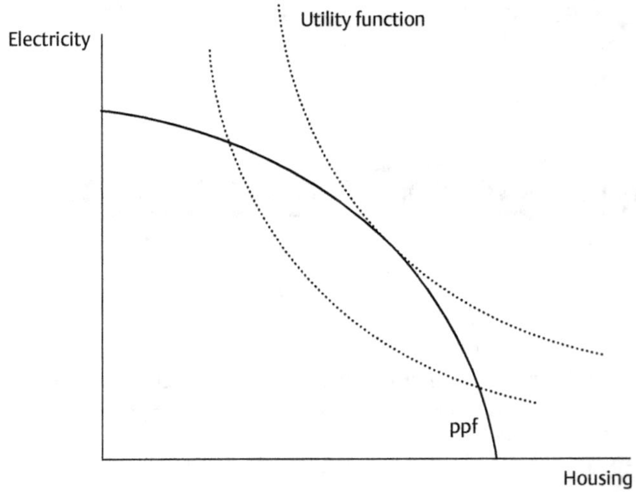

Question 9.3*

Suppose that the German government allows a Danish electricity firm to supply electricity to the German consumers and compete with the German monopolist (see question 9.2). Transport costs to the German market are negligible for this Danish firm. We analyse the new situation with the assistance of the figure for question 9.3, depicting an isoprofit curve for both the Danish firm and the German firm.

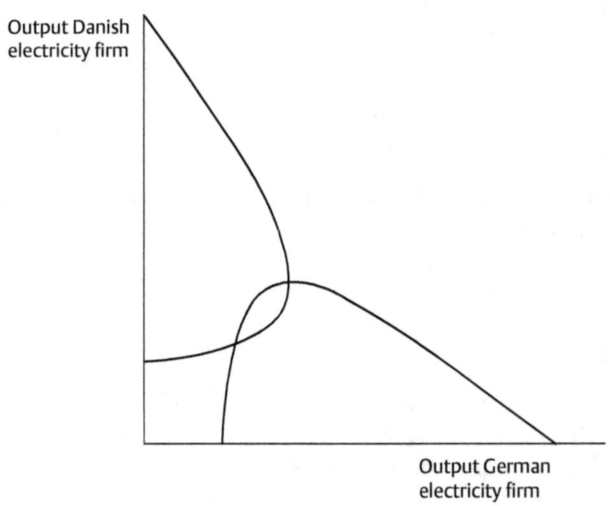

A. What is an isoprofit curve and what is a reaction curve? Draw the reaction curve of the German electricity firm in the figure above. Also indicate which isoprofit curve belongs to which firm.

B. Indicate in the same figure the output levels that result in a situation of monopoly and the output levels that result in a situation of perfect competition (in which you assume that price is equal to marginal cost) on the German electricity market.

C. Indicate in the figure the output levels of the German firm and the Danish firm in a situation of Cournot oligopoly. Explain why this is an equilibrium.

D. In questions 9.3B and 9.3C you have marked the output levels under perfect competition, monopoly, and Cournot oligopoly in one figure. Compare these output levels. Which market situation gives the largest output?

Question 9.4

Most economic reforms within countries result in winners and losers. Changing the German electricity market from a situation of monopoly to a situation of oligopoly by allowing the Danish electricity firm to compete on the market (see question 9.3) is no exception to this rule.

A. What will the German electricity firm, which initially was the monopoly producer, think of the economic reform in the German electricity market?

B. What will the Danish electricity firm, which was granted access to the German electricity market, think of the economic reform?

C. What will German consumers think of the reform?

Question 9.5

Let us analyse the gains and losses associated with the entry of the Danish electricity firm on the German market more formally (see questions 9.2–9.4). Recall that there was initially only a German monopoly producer on the market. In the new situation a Danish firm is also allowed to sell electricity in Germany. The figure for question 9.5 gives the demand for electricity in Germany and the marginal revenue curve for the German monopolist in the initial situation.

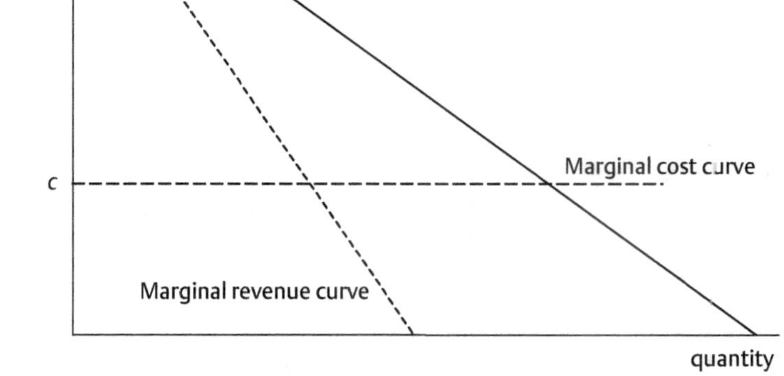

A. What are the consumer surplus and producer surplus in a situation of monopoly?

B. Indicate (in the same figure) a possible total quantity of electricity supplied and the associated price level if the Danish firm is allowed to compete on the German market. Assume that there are no transport costs.

C. What is the consumer surplus and producer surplus in this new situation?

D. Who gains and who loses from the entry of the Danish firm?

E. What are the pro-competitive gains from trade?

Assume now that the Danish firm faces *positive* transport costs when delivering electricity to the German market. We assume that it is still profitable for the Danish firm to supply electricity to German consumers.

F. Indicate in the same figure a possible total quantity of electricity supplied and the associated price level if the Danish firm faces positive transport costs. Make sure your figure is consistent with your earlier answers.

G. Who gains and who loses from the entry of the Danish firm if there are positive transport costs? Are the gains and losses equal to the situation without transport costs? Explain.

Empirical questions

Question 9.6

Historically, the market for electricity is characterized by oligopolistic firms. Since the 1980s a number of European countries have tried to promote competition on their electricity markets. It is interesting to see if these regulatory reforms have increased consumption and trade in electricity between the European countries. In the 'question 9-6' Excel file on the website you can find consumption, import, export, and production data of electricity for various European countries. In addition, the file contains a table indicating the degree of openness of the electricity market in these countries. Does a larger degree of market openness lead to more consumption and trade in electricity? Interpret your results.

Question 9.7

China has entered the World Trade Organization in 2001.[1] One of the conditions for entry is easier access to the Chinese market for foreign competitors. This will, of course, have an impact on the structure of the Chinese economy. Search the internet for information about the impact of a Chinese membership to the WTO

[1] See Chapter 12 for more information about this organization.

for different Chinese industries. What are the positive and/or negative changes for these industries? Evaluate the arguments you encounter using the analysis of Chapter 9.

Simulation questions

Question 9.8*

The 'question 9-8' Excel file on the website repeats Figure 9.5 of the book. There are two firms, A and B. In the reciprocal dumping model of Chapter 9 it was assumed that both firms face the same marginal costs and only one firm has to incur transport costs. The simulation is slightly more flexible in this respect. It allows you to change the marginal costs and transport costs of both firms. It is important to note that the transport costs are of the iceberg type.

Assume that in the initial situation, firm A produces for the domestic market. Hence, it does not have to incur any transport costs to sell its products. Firm B is a foreign producer, selling on the domestic market. The transport costs are very high for this firm. Only half of the goods that are sent from B's plant arrive in the domestic market (transport cost parameter $T = 2$). Both firms face a marginal cost equal to unity.

A. Simulate the initial situation (the numbers currently entered in the simulation are incorrect). What are the output and profit levels of both firms? Explain the differences between the two firms.

B. If you increase the marginal costs of firm A, what happens to the reaction and isoprofit curves of firms A and B?

C. If you increase the transport costs that firm A has to incur, what happens to the reaction and isoprofit curves of firms A and B?

D. Compare your answers to questions 9.8B and 9.8C. Explain the differences and similarities.

The domestic government is considering building a road which reduces the transport costs for foreign firms.

E. Decrease the transport costs of firm B. What is the effect of this decrease on the quantities supplied and the profits of firms A and B? Explain.

F. Will firm A and B be in favour of building the road?

G. What is the effect of the decrease of transport costs of firm B, on total quantity supplied and the price level? Explain.

H. Will the consumers on the domestic market be in favour of building the road?

Technical questions

Question 9.9

Suppose that a market is characterized by the following demand function:

$$p = a - bQ$$

where p is the price level, Q the total quantity supplied on this market, and a and b are parameter constants. Furthermore, it is given that all firms face the same constant marginal cost of production.

A. What quantity will a monopolist supply? What is the price level (p) and what is the total quantity (Q) supplied to the market?

B. Suppose that two firms are active on the market. What quantity will a Cournot oligopolist supply in equilibrium? What is the price level and what is the total quantity supplied to the market?

C. Compare the price level and total quantity supplied in a situation of monopoly and a situation of oligopoly.

D. Suppose there are N symmetric firms. What quantity will an individual firm supply in Cournot equilibrium? What is the price level and what is the total quantity supplied to the market?

E. What happens with the price level and total quantity supplied if you increase N? Explain.

Question 9.10

Suppose again (see question 9.9) that all firms face the same constant marginal cost of production and the market demand function is equal to:

$$p = a - bQ$$

where p is the price level, Q the total quantity supplied on this market, and a and b are parameter constants. In question 9.5 you were asked to draw the consumer surplus and producer surplus in one figure. In this question we derive these surpluses mathematically.

A. Define the consumer surplus as a function of Q. What happens if you increase Q?

B. Define the producer surplus as a function of Q. What happens if you increase Q?

C. Define the total surplus as a function of Q. What happens if you increase Q?

Question 9.11

As in questions 9.9 and 9.10, we assume that the demand function is linear: $p = a - bQ$. Suppose there are two firms, A and B, facing different constant marginal costs

(c_A and c_B) and different iceberg transport costs (T_A and T_B). Both firms compete with each other by setting quantities.

A. Calculate the reaction curves of both firms.

B. What is the quantity each firm will supply in Cournot equilibrium? What is the price of the good on the market in Cournot equilibrium?

C. What is the effect of a change in T_A on your answers to question 9.11B?

10

Intra-industry Trade

Chapter 10 analyses imperfect competition in combination with economies of scale and shows that the size of the market determines the number of different types of goods and services available. Trade increases the extent of the market, thus making more types of goods available. This can be used to explain the empirical phenomenon of intra-industry trade (two-way trade in similar types of goods).

Review questions

Question 10.1

A. Section 10.3 discusses the Dixit–Stiglitz model of monopolistic competition. The parameter ρ is said to represent the love-of-variety effect. What is the love-of-variety effect and why do we need it to explain intra-industry trade?

B. Section 10.4 of the book discusses the demand for a particular variety of manufactures, in particular the importance of the parameter ε. Which different economic forces does the parameter ε represent in the Dixit–Stiglitz model?

C. How does the Dixit–Stiglitz model of imperfect competition deviate from perfect competition models?

Question 10.2

Chapter 10 introduces the Constant Elasticity of Substitution (CES) utility function. Suppose that a consumer with this type of utility function (see equation 10.2) consumes three goods: coffee, tea, and milk.

A. Use a numerical example to show that if $\rho = 1$ the consumer is indifferent to consuming three units of coffee or three units of a mix of the goods.

B. Use a numerical example to show that if $0 < \rho < 1$ the consumer prefers to purchase a combination of goods.

For the rest of this question we assume that each good is consumed in the same quantity. Section 10.3 then rewrites the utility function to distinguish between a love-of-variety effect and a claim on real resources (see equation 10.2′). Suppose that $\rho = 0.5$ and assume that one unit of each good is consumed.

C. Rewrite the utility function for coffee, tea, and milk to mimic equation (10.2′). How large is the claim on real resources? How large is the love-of-variety effect?

D. Use an example to illustrate how the love-of-variety effect represents a multiplier-like role in the utility function (use quation 10.2′).

Question 10.3

Give a real-world example of:

A. Pure external economies of scale

B. Pecuniary external economies of scale

C. Internal economies of scale

Question10.4*

Suppose we live in a Dixit–Stiglitz world as described in Chapter 10 with three car producers, called Ferrari, Lamborghini, and Porsche, and the following parameters:

$$p_{Porsche} = 10; \quad p_{Lamborghini} = 5; \quad p_{Ferrari} = 10$$

$$\rho = 0.5; \quad I = 100; \quad P = 2.5$$

Suppose that the producers have a fixed labour input of 5 and a variable labour input of 1. They face a wage rate of 1 and the labour force consists of 50 workers.

A. Is the model currently in equilibrium (use equation (10.9))?

B. How many cars are produced in equilibrium by a single car manufacturer? How much labour is used to produce this output (use equation (10.8))?

C. How many car varieties will be sold in equilibrium in this market? What will be the output of the three car manufacturers if new producers can enter the market?

D. The monopolistic competition analysis in this question is subject to one of the theoretical problems mentioned in the book. What is this problem?

Question 10.5

China and Australia both produce fireworks. The demand and supply structure in both economies is given by the Dixit–Stiglitz model, with an elasticity of substitution equal to 2 in both countries. Since continually firing the same crackers is quite boring, there is a love-of-variety effect for all consumers. The fireworks market is much larger in China than in Australia. In both countries the marginal labour input requirement is 1 and the fixed labour input per variety is 2.5. The Chinese labour employment in the fireworks industry is 10 million people. The Australian labour employment in the fireworks industry is 10,000 people.

A. How many varieties will be supplied to the Australian and Chinese market in the autarky equilibrium?

B. How many varieties will be consumed in each country in the free trade equilibrium?

C. Does international trade increase the production efficiency in the two countries? Does international trade increase output?

D. What is the domestic market share of Australian producers if international trade is allowed?

Read the following statement:

> Opening up the Australian market for fireworks to free trade with China will result in a drastic decline of the domestic market share for Australian producers. Since this is not in their interest, these producers can be expected to lobby the Australian parliament for tariffs on Chinese fireworks.

E. Comment on the above statement.

F. What happens to the wages of Australian and Chinese workers under free trade?

G. Who benefits and who loses from international trade in this model?

Question 10.6

The intra-industry trade model can be interpreted in two ways: the Krugman and Ethier interpretations.

A. Which interpretation of the model have we used in question 10.5?

B. What are the main differences between the Krugman interpretation and the Ethier interpretation?

C. What is the result of an increase in the extent of the market in the Ethier interpretation?

D. What was the main motivation for Ethier to reinterpret the Krugman intra-industry trade model?

Question 10.7*

The Krugman and Ethier interpretations of intra-industry trade are not exclusive.

A. Draw a figure such as 10.7 or 10.8 in which you integrate the Krugman and Ethier interpretations. Assume that there are two countries each producing two intermediate and two final goods.

B. In what ways is free trade advantageous for the two countries?

Empirical questions

Question 10.8

The 'question 10-8' Excel file on the website contains import and export data for aggregate manufactures and five sectors for the NAFTA and the EU.

A. Calculate the Grubel–Lloyd index for all sectors in the dataset.

B. Display the development of the Grubel–Lloyd index over time for all sectors in a graph.

C. Which sector fits the predictions of the neoclassical trade model best? Why?

D. Which interpretation of the intra-industry trade model (Krugman or Ethier) do you prefer to explain intra-industry trade for iron and steel? Why?

Simulation questions

Question 10.9

The 'question 10-9' simulation on the website describes the demand and supply of luxury cars in the European Union. The simulation consists of two sections: the demand side of the model and the supply side, respectively. We start with the demand section, in which the consumer maximizes utility by changing the consumption levels, taking the price as given.

A new feature of MS Excel, the 'solver', has to be introduced before one can start with the simulation. This solver is capable of solving a system of equations by substituting in rapid pace different values in the equations and selecting the values that solve the system. You can start the solver in MS Excel by clicking 'solver' in the tools menu. The solver is already programmed so you just have to push the 'solve' button. After a few seconds a new window appears which tells you whether the solution has been found or not. Pushing 'OK' will return you to the simulation.

Another thing you will have to take into account is that by starting up the simulation your computer will ask you whether you want to enable or disable macros. For the simulation to work properly you will have to enable the macros.

The simulation starts at a price of six for all three types of cars. Note that some of the values have to be changed before you can answer the questions below.

A. Change the price of one of the three cars and run the simulation. What happens to consumption and the price index? Why?

B. Increase the love-of-variety effect and run the simulation. What happens to consumption? What is the economic intuition for this?

C. Now decrease the elasticity of substitution and run the simulation. What happens to the consumption levels? What is the economic intuition for this?

D. Which demand side factor influences the number of varieties on the market in equilibrium? Can you explain why?

The supply side of the Dixit–Stiglitz model is modelled on the 'supply' worksheet in the Excel file. The model is initially in equilibrium. The simulation ensures that the industry-wide profits become zero, given the prices you have imposed.

E. Increase the price of one of the varieties and run the simulation. What happens to the profits of the three manufacturers? Is this an equilibrium situation?

F. Can the prices for the different varieties deviate from each other in equilibrium? Why, or why not?

G. Make the price equal to 6 for each car, decrease the variable labour input and run the simulation again. What happens to production? Do the producers have an incentive to change their prices?

Suppose now that we have an identical model of the Japanese car market, with the manufacturers Toyota, Mitsubishi, and Honda. The initially closed European car market now opens up to Japanese suppliers and vice versa. Answer the questions below without performing any simulations.

H. What happens to the production levels of the car types in the European Union?

I. Which trade flows do you expect to arise (who exports what)?

Technical questions

Question 10.10

In the Dixit–Stiglitz model the prices are the same for every variety in equilibrium.

A. Rewrite and simplify the price index of the model given this information.

B. Show that with the price index you have calculated in question 10.10A the consumption of a variety *in equilibrium* simplifies to: $c_j = I/p_j[N^{(1-\varepsilon)(\varepsilon-1)}]$

C. Income is defined as $\sum_{i=1}^{N} p_i c_i$. Given that all prices are equal and consumption levels are equal, rewrite income as a function of the number of varieties.

D. Use equation (10.A5) and your results of questions 10.10B and 10.10C to arrive at the same outcome as in equation (10.2).

11

Strategic Trade Policy

Chapter 11 analyses the impact of 'strategic' trade policy, designed to give domestic producers an advantage in a world characterized by imperfect competition.

Review questions

Question 11.1 *

In the state of Alusia there is only one producer of olive oil. The producer is highly regarded by the government of Alusia because it has been producing olive oil for centuries using traditional methods which give the olive oil a typical Alusian taste. After a long period of autarky the Alusian government decides to open the borders for international trade and allow its citizens to consume a larger variety of products. The government is, however, concerned about the consequences of this policy for the olive oil monopolist. The figure for question 11.1 gives the demand for olive oil in Alusia, the marginal cost curve of the monopolist, and the price of olive oil on the world markets.

A. Indicate the autarky quantity supplied to the market and the price of olive oil in the figure above.

B. What would be the production level of olive oil for the Alusian producer, the quantity imported, and the price of olive oil in Alusia under free trade?

The Alusian government is considering imposing a tariff on the imports of olive oil.

C. Determine for every potential level of the tariff rate, the domestic production level, the import level, and the price level. Indicate these levels in the figure.

D. Consider for every level of the tariff rate, the consumer surplus and the producer surplus. Indicate these surpluses in the figure.

E. Which tariff rate should the government impose if it wants to maximize the total surplus?

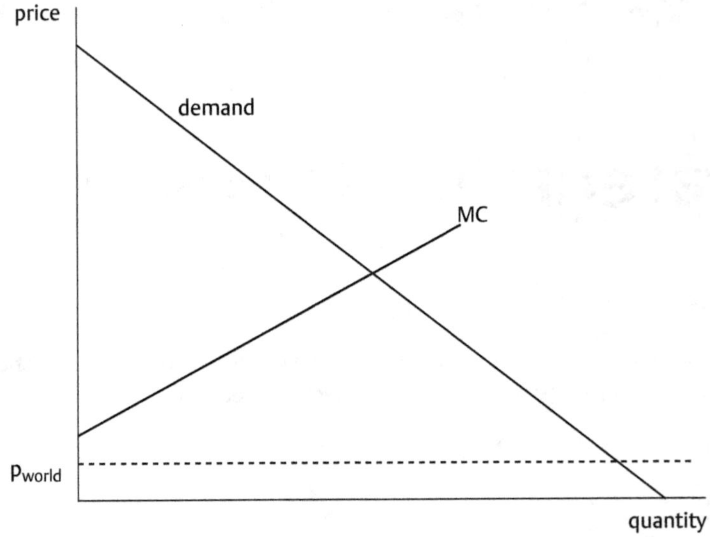

Question 11.2

The government of Alusia is not sure if the analysis in question 11.1 is correct. In particular, it is not sure if the domestic producer of olive oil faces an increasing marginal cost curve.

A. Draw the figure given in question 11.1 with a constant marginal cost curve.

B. Consider the effects of a tariff under the assumption of constant marginal costs. What would be the domestic production level, the import level, and the price level for every possible tariff rate? Indicate these levels in the figure.

C. Draw the figure given in question 11.1 again, this time with a decreasing marginal cost curve.

D. At which price level does a producer make no profit or loss?

E. Consider the effects of a tariff under the assumption of decreasing marginal costs. What would be domestic production, the level of imports, and the price level for every possible tariff level? Indicate these levels in the figure assuming that the marginal cost curve intersects the demand curve above the world price.

Question 11.3

Tariffs are not the only means to protect the industry of a country, as also recognized by the government of Alusia (see question 11.1), which is now considering protecting the domestic olive oil producer with an import quota on olive oil. Use the figure of question 11.1 to answer the questions below.

A. What will be the price and quantity on the market if a quota is introduced? Indicate your answer in a new figure.

B. What price will foreign producers charge for their olive oil?

C. Do you think the foreign producers are content with the quota?

D. Indicate the consumer surplus and the surplus of the monopolist if a quota is introduced.

Question 11.4

Questions 11.1 and 11.3 deal with the consequences of imposing a tariff or a quota on the Alusian olive oil market without giving clear policy recommendations.

A. Suppose that the objective of the Alusian government is to maximize consumer surplus. Do you recommend the Alusian government impose a tariff or a quota? How high should the tariff or quota be?

B. Suppose that the objective of the Alusian government is to maximize the surplus of the domestic producer. Do you recommend the Alusian government impose a tariff or a quota? How high should the tariff or quota be?

C. Suppose that the objective of the Alusian government is to maximize the total surplus. Do you recommend the Alusian government impose a tariff or a quota? How high should the tariff or quota be?

Question 11.5

Chapter 11 describes two different oligopoly situations.

A. What is the main difference between a Cournot oligopoly and a Bertrand oligopoly?

B. Comparing Figures 11.4 and 11.5 of the book it is clear that the reaction curve under Cournot competition is negatively sloped, while under Bertrand competition it is positively sloped. How do you explain this difference?

C. When comparing Figures 11.4 and 11.5 if is also clear that the isoprofit curve of firm A is turned around 180 degrees. How do you explain this difference?

Question 11.6

After the financial crisis in 1997, the economies of the South-East Asian countries are growing rapidly again. The economic growth is likely to be accompanied by a growth in air travels. Large opportunities exist for both Boeing and Airbus to sell their planes in South-East Asia. Let us analyse the market for large aeroplanes in South-East Asia using the Cournot framework. The figure for question 11.6 gives possible reaction curves and isoprofit curves for both Airbus and Boeing.

A. Indicate for each of the different curves if it is a reaction curve or an isoprofit curve and to which of the two firms it belongs.

B. Chapter 9 shows that the Cournot equilibrium outcome is point *a*. However, at point *b* Airbus has a higher profit level. Explain carefully why the equilibrium outcome is not at point *b*.

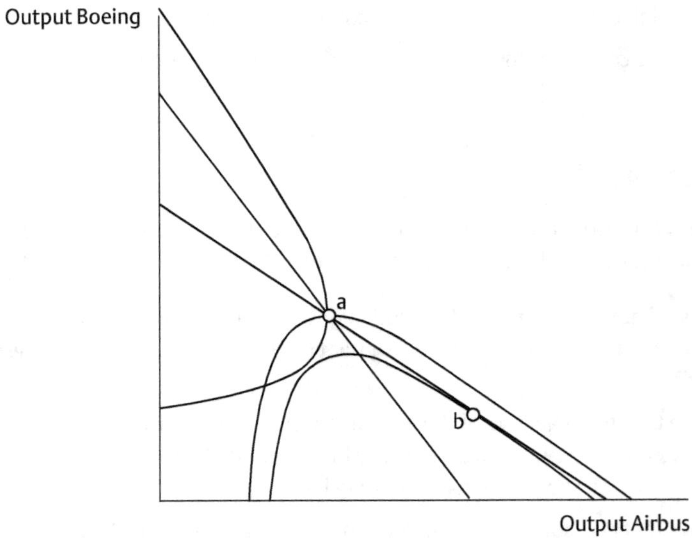

Suppose that the European Commission would like to give Airbus a strategic advantage in the South-East Asian region. It therefore gives an optimal (total welfare maximizing) subsidy for every aeroplane Airbus sells to the South-East Asian region.

C. Draw the new situation in the figure above. What are the new output levels for both firms and how does the output of both firms change?

D. What will the US government think of this EU subsidy? Use the new figure to explain their position.

The US government enviously looks at the European subsidy and decides to also impose an optimal subsidy, given the EU subsidy.

E. Draw the situation that arises after the imposition of the US subsidy in the figure. What are the new output levels of both firms?

F. What will the EU government think of this US subsidy? Is it rational for the European Commission to react?

G. Assume that the European Commission sets a new optimal subsidy, followed by the US setting an optimal subsidy, followed by the EU again etc. Will both countries eventually be better off or worse off?

Question 11.7

We could also imagine that Airbus and Boeing (see question 11.6) are competing with each other in a Bertrand framework (price competition), rather than a Cournot framework (quantity competition).

A. Draw the reaction curves and some isoprofit curves for both Airbus and Boeing in a Bertrand framework. Put the price of an Airbus aircraft on the horizontal axis and the price of a Boeing aircraft on the vertical axis.

The European Commission again wants to stimulate Airbus sales in South-East Asia.

B. Should the European Commission subsidize or tax the aircraft Airbus sells to South-East Asia? Explain why.

C. Suppose the European Commission optimally employs the instrument of question 11.7B. Draw the new situation in the figure. How does the price demanded for aircraft change for both Airbus and Boeing?

D. What will the US government think of the EU policy? Why?

E. Do you think the Bertrand framework is appropriate to analyse retaliation between governments?

Empirical questions

Question 11.8

Since the Second World War, the Japanese government has targeted the development of specific industries, mainly under the direction of MITI (Ministry of International Trade and Industry).[1] Strategic trade policy is one of the means by which the development of these specific industries has been encouraged. Search the internet for information on the trade policy of MITI after the Second World War. Which industries were targeted? What kind of trade related measures were taken to encourage the development of industries? How successful has the trade policy been for Japan?

Simulation questions

Question 11.9

Consider two aircraft producers, Airbus and Boeing, selling their product to a third market, South-East Asia. The firms are in Cournot competition, such that their situation can be simulated with the help of Figure 11.4 in the book. The 'question 11-9' Excel file on the website repeats this figure and allows you to change the marginal cost of the aircraft producers and the export subsidies awarded by the two governments.

[1] Since January 2001 this ministry is called METI (Ministry of Economy, Trade, and Industry).

The simulation has the starting values: $c_a = c_b = 1$ and $s_a = s_b = 0$. Note that some of the values in the simulation have to be changed before you can answer the questions below.

A. What happens to the output and profit levels if you decrease the marginal costs of Airbus? What happens to the output and profit levels if you increase the subsidy to Airbus by an equal amount, starting from the same initial situation? Compare both results and explain your observations.

The US government contemplates giving an export subsidy to Boeing to improve its competitive position in South-East Asia.

B. Starting from the initial situation, fill in the table below.

US subsidy	1	2	3	4	5	6	7	8
Boeing profits								
Total subsidy received								

C. At which subsidy level is the Brander–Spencer equilibrium reached? Explain.

D. What will the European Commission think of the imposition of an optimal subsidy by the US government?

E. What is the optimal subsidy level the European Commission could impose in response to the US subsidy?

F. Compare the situation of no subsidies with the situation in which both governments have imposed their optimal subsidies. Did the policy of giving subsidies lead to a higher welfare in the two regions?

G. What do consumers in the South-East Asian market think of the subsidies by both governments? Explain.

Question 11.10

Airbus and Boeing could also be in Bertrand competition on the South-East Asian market. The 'question 11-10' Excel file on the website repeats Figure 11.5 of the book and allows you to change the constant marginal costs and the export tax for both aeroplane producers.

The simulation has the starting values: $c_a = c_b = 1$ and $t_a = t_b = 0$. Note that some of the values in the simulation have to be changed before you can answer the questions below.

A. What happens to the price and profit levels if you increase the marginal cost of Airbus? What happens to the price and profit levels if you increase the Airbus tax by an equal amount, starting from the same initial situation? Compare both results and explain your observations.

The US government plans to introduce a tax for Boeing to improve the strategic position of Boeing in the South-East Asian region.

B. Starting from the initial situation, fill in the table below.

US tax	0	1	2	3	4	5	6	7	8
Boeing profits									
Total tax paid									

C. At which tax level is the Eaton–Grossman equilibrium reached?

D. Does Boeing gain from the introduction of a tax by the US government? Does the US government gain from this tax?

E. Does Airbus gain from the introduction of a tax by the US government?

F. Do the consumers in South-East Asia gain from the introduction of the tax by the US government?

Technical questions

Question 11.11*

Chapter 9 analysed a monopoly producer in a market with a linear demand function $p = a - bQ$ facing a constant marginal cost c. This question considers the effect of a quota on the behaviour of the monopolist.

A. Specify the demand function after the introduction of a quota.

B. Calculate the optimal price and output for the monopolist, given the quota level.

Question 11.12

Two firms, A and B, are competing with each other in Cournot style on a third market with a linear demand function: $p = a - bQ$, where p is the price, Q the total output by both firms, and a and b are parameter constants. The two firms are located in different countries, also called A and B. The governments of these countries can award an export subsidy (s_A and s_B) per unit of product transported to the third market. Both firms face the same per unit marginal costs c.

A. Calculate the equilibrium output levels for both firms, given the subsidy levels.

B. Express the equilibrium profits of both firms in terms of s_A and s_B.

C. What is the optimal subsidy for government A, given the subsidy level s_B?

D. What are the profits for both firms if s_A is set to its optimal level (as you derived in question 11.12C)?

E. Suppose initially that $s_A = s_B = 0$. Government A now introduces an optimal subsidy. Show mathematically which firm gains and which firm loses.

Question 11.13

In a Bertrand model with two firms, A and B, competing with each other on a third market the demand functions for the products of these two firms are given by:

$$q_A = a - p_A + p_B$$

$$q_B = a - p_B + p_A$$

where q_i is the output of each firm, p_i the price demanded, and a is a parameter. The firms are located in different countries, also called A and B, where the governments have the opportunity to impose an export tax (t_A and t_B) per unit of product shipped to the third market. Both firms face per unit marginal costs c.

A. From your microeconomics textbook you are probably used to the Bertrand game where the products of both firms are perfect substitutes. Is this also the case in this set-up of the Bertrand model?

B. What are the reaction curves for both firms?

C. What are the equilibrium price levels of both goods, given the export taxes of both governments?

D. Express the equilibrium profits of both firms in terms of t_A and t_B.

E. What is the optimal tax for the government of country A, given t_B?

F. What are the equilibrium profits of both firms if t_A is set to its optimal level (as derived in question 11.13E)?

G. Suppose initially that $t_A = t_B = 0$. Government A now introduces an optimal tax. Show mathematically which firm gains and which firm loses.

12

International Trade Organizations

Chapter 12 discusses the history and functioning of the main international trade organizations.

Review questions

Question 12.1

The world has recently witnessed the rise of a new movement vehemently opposed to international bodies such as the World Bank, the IMF, and the WTO. As described in Box 12.1, this movement consists of many different groups of people, usually opposing different elements of the economic developments in the world. In view of this discontent, which apparently makes people so angry that they are willing to smash city centres, break windows, start fires, and fight with the police, it is good to discuss some of the many issues raised by the protestors. For clarity, we focus the discussion on the WTO as it is the most important trade organization and was the first target of the demonstrators. Give your view on the claims below.

- The WTO is an undemocratic organization.
- The WTO promotes international trade that is bad for the environment.
- The WTO exclusively represents the interests of the developed nations and the multinationals.
- The WTO leads to the development of a monotone global culture which destroys the diversity of other cultures.
- The WTO promotes 'unfair' trade.
- WTO policies increase global inequality.
- The WTO policy of free trade destroys jobs.

Question 12.2

The case study in section 12.5 describes the transition process of Central and Eastern European countries. Figure 12.7 gives an overview of the possible economic systems countries may choose.

A. State for each of the countries below in which corner of Figure 12.7 you would place the country.
- Germany
- USA
- China
- Cuba

Figure 12.8 describes the hypothetical transition of one of the Eastern European countries to capitalism.

B. Can you explain why the relative price is different before and after the transition process?

Empirical questions

Question 12.3

Go to the website of the WTO at http://www.wto.org where you can find the answers to the following questions.

A. What are the main objectives of the WTO?

B. How is the WTO trying to achieve these objectives?

Question 12.4

Nations frequently clash with each other on various trade issues, often charging the other side with 'dumping' practices. On the website of the WTO you can find answers to the following questions.

A. What is the definition of 'dumping'? What is the stance of the WTO towards countries which protect themselves from 'dumping' practices?

B. What are anti-dumping measures called in WTO terminology? What measures can you think of that policy makers would implement?

Question 12.5

An important and controversial treaty agreed upon at the WTO is the issue of intellectual property rights. The WTO's Agreement on Trade Related Aspects of Intellectual

Property Rights (TRIPs) is the official name of the WTO treaty that handles these rights. Go to the website of the WTO to answer the questions below.

A. Which broad issues with respect to intellectual property rights are covered by the TRIPs agreement?

B. Why do intellectual property rights need to be discussed at a global level?

C. Which special arrangements have been made for developing countries in the TRIPs agreement? Why?

The TRIPs agreement has drawn a lot of criticism. Many people claim that it will be bad for developing nations and good for developed nations.

D. Can you think of reasons why the TRIPs agreement would be bad for developing countries? And reasons why it would be good?

Pharmaceutical companies have been criticized recently for their hesitation to supply cheap AIDS medicines to developing countries, as well as for their attempts to block the production of cheap copies of such medicines in the developing countries. The TRIPs agreement will have a big impact on this issue.

E. Why is it beneficial for developing countries to produce the drugs cheaply in their own country? Why can it be detrimental?

Question 12.6

A well-organized anti-globalization website, with many links to other sites and articles explaining their position on the global economy, is provided by global exchange, see http://www.globalexchange.org.

A. There are many reasons to oppose the WTO according to this website. Mention three arguments as given on the site and comment on these arguments.

B. A large section of the site is dedicated to 'fair' trade. What problems can you raise concerning the issue of 'fair' trade?

Question 12.7

On the UNCTAD website, see http://www.unctad.org, you can find answers to the questions below.

A. What are the main objectives of UNCTAD?

B. How is UNCTAD trying to achieve these objectives?

As explained in the book, the World Investment Report is currently the most important UNCTAD publication, containing a wealth of information on global investment. The report is available online at the UNCTAD website.

C. What are the main trends of FDI (foreign direct investment) according to the most recent World Investment Report?

D. Which countries are the biggest recipients and the biggest sources of FDI flows?

E. Which developing nation is the largest recipient of FDI?

F. Which nations host the largest multinational corporations?

Question 12.8

The website of the International Trade Centre offers a wealth of information to the economic researcher. You can find detailed statistics on almost all countries in the world. Choose a country of your interest and answer the following questions. You can find the answers to these questions by choosing the country approach and picking your preferred country on the website (http://www.intracen.org).

A. What are the most important export products of your country?

B. What type of goods does your country tend to export if you look at the factor intensities?

C. In which sectors does your country have a 'revealed' comparative advantage?

Question 12.9

The Organization for Economic Cooperation and Development (OECD) is the last important international trade organization discussed in the book. It is best known for its publications, its extensive data set for the member states, and its role as a forum for developed nations. On its website http://www.oecd.org, you will find the information needed to answer the questions below.

A. In the 1980s and 1990s there was a strong political discussion in the United States about the trade deficit with Japan. Find the trade statistics on the website and graph the development of the US trade deficit with Japan over the available years.

B. More recently the rising trade deficit with China has drawn the attention of the American Congress. Graph the development of the American trade deficit with China over the available years.

13

Economic Integration

Chapter 13 reviews some preferential trade agreements, with special attention for Europe and EU enlargement. The rising popularity of economic integration, known as 'regionalism', is discussed in a neoclassical model and in a new trade framework.

Review questions

Question 13.1

In the figure for question 13.1 the demand for and the supply of clothes in Singapore are given by $D_{Singapore}$ and $S_{Singapore}$, respectively. The horizontal supply curves S_{China} and S_{India} represent the supply of clothes from China and India when Singapore does not impose any tariffs on these imports. The horizontal supply curves S'_{China} and S'_{India} represent the supply from China and India if Singapore imposes a tariff to all imports, as it does initially.

A. From which country does Singapore import clothes in the initial situation? Explain why the imports come from this country.

B. Indicate the price of clothes in Singapore, the quantity of clothes produced in Singapore, and the imports of clothes into Singapore in the figure overleaf.

Suppose the government of Singapore is considering establishing a customs union with China or with India.

C. What happens to imports, the price of clothes in Singapore, and the production in Singapore if Singapore establishes a customs union with China?

D. What are the trade creation and trade diversion effects of a customs union with China?

E. What are the welfare effects of a customs union with China for consumers, producers, and the government of Singapore? What is the total welfare effect?

F. What happens to imports, the price of clothes in Singapore, and the production in Singapore if Singapore establishes a customs union with India?

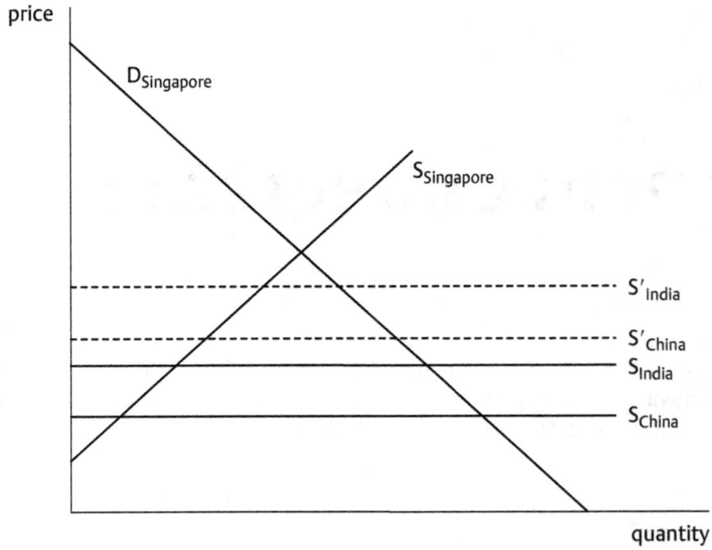

G. What are the trade creation and trade diversion effects of a customs union with India?

H. What are the welfare effects for Singapore of a customs union with India?

I. What happens to imports, the price of clothes in Singapore, and the production in Singapore if Singapore establishes a customs union with both China and India? What are the welfare effects?

Question 13.2*

Figure 13.3 in the book describes a situation in which a customs union leads to trade diversion. As explained in the text this type of customs union can either lead to a positive or a negative welfare effect. Look carefully at Figure 13.3 and explain which economic forces (prices and/or elasticities) are mainly responsible for a negative welfare effect.

Question 13.3

The two questions above have looked at economic integration from a partial equilibrium perspective. This question focuses on a general equilibrium perspective.

A. What do Kemp and Wan predict for the welfare of the world as a whole if some countries form a customs union?

B. What does Krugman predict in the regionalism model for the welfare of the world as a whole if some countries form a customs union?

C. Explain the differences and/or similarities in your answers to questions 13.3A and 13.3B.

Question 13.4

Chapter 13 of the book gives an overview of the establishment of the European Union, at present the most successful region of economic integration. It is important to realize that Europe went through several stages of economic integration before it reached the current state of affairs. Write an essay describing these different stages of economic integration, noting when and how the EU entered each new stage.

Empirical questions

Question 13.5.

Based on the trade creation and trade diversion arguments of section 13.3 of the book, one would expect that the creation of a customs union will increase the international trade flows between the member countries. We will analyse this for a particular member of the European Union: Belgium/Luxembourg. The 'question 13-5' Excel file on the website contains data on imports into Belgium/Luxembourg from different member states of the European Union from 1960 to 1998. Use these data to analyse whether the enlargement of the European Union with new members has increased the trade between Belgium/Luxembourg and these new members.

Question 13.6

Regional trade agreements differ considerably in the extent to which members trade with each other. Go to the websites of the different regional trade agreements mentioned in Chapter 13 and try to determine the extent of the trade intensity of some of these regional trade agreements.

Question 13.7

Chapter 13 reviews some of the more important regional trade agreements. Many other agreements exist. Search the internet for other regional trade agreements for the region in the world where you are currently reading this study guide. Which countries participate in this agreement? What type of regional integration does it encompass?

Technical questions

Question 13.8

Assume that the world consists of N countries, each country being of equal size and each country producing a different variety of a product. The demand for a variety is given by (see Chapter 10 for a detailed explanation of this demand function):

$$c_j = p_j^{-\varepsilon} P^{\varepsilon-1} Y \quad \text{in which } P = \left[\sum_{i=1}^{N} p_i^{1-\varepsilon}\right]^{1/(1-\varepsilon)}$$

where c_j is the demand for variety j, p_j the price of variety j, P the price index for all varieties together, Y the income level of a country and ε the elasticity of substitution.

The N countries can form b different trading blocks. For simplicity we assume that these trading blocks consist of an equal number of countries. Within such a trading block, countries trade their goods for a price of one. A tariff is levied on trade with other trading blocks. Consumers in a country therefore pay a price equal to 1 for products coming from countries within the same trading block and a price equal to $1 + t$ for products coming from countries of other trading blocks.

A. Rewrite the price index in terms of N, b, t and ε.

B. What is the total demand for a variety (c_j) expressed in Y, N, b, t and ε?

C. What is the income of one country if you assume $c_j = 1$?

D. What is the world welfare if you assume $c_j = 1$.

Part IV

New Interactions

14

Geographical Economics

Chapter 14 presents a simple general equilibrium model of location by combining factor mobility with some of the insights of the neoclassical trade model and the new trade model. This allows us to explain some empirical observations (such as Zipf's Law and the gravity equation).

Review questions

Question 14.1

Figure 14.4 of the book, which is replicated here, summarizes the structure of the geographical economics model.

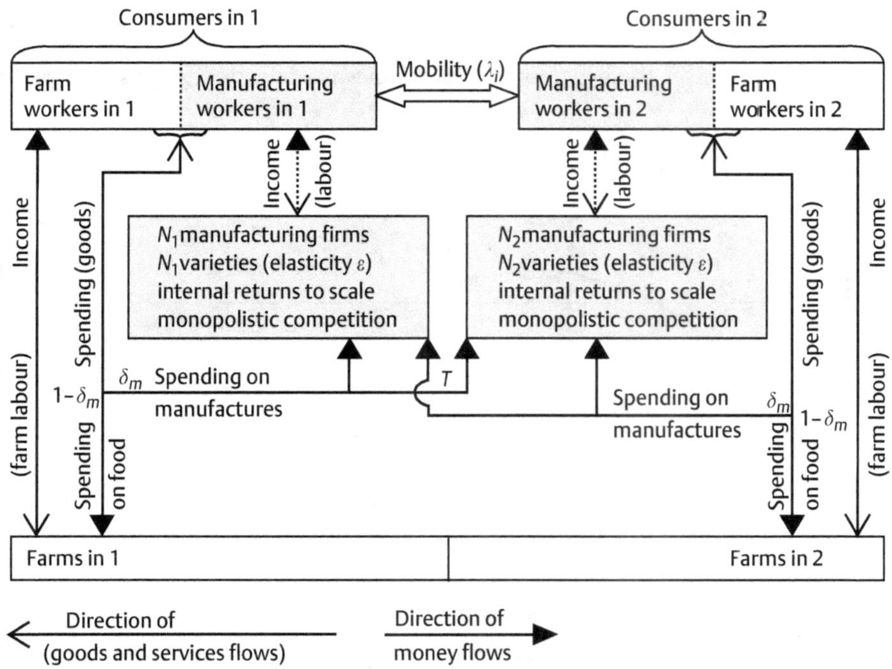

A. Who are the different economic agents in the geographical economics model?

B. Determine for every agent whether he or she is active on the demand side or the supply side of the model.

C. Determine for every agent which actions he or she can take in the model.

D. Determine for every agent which decisions he or she has to make in the model.

Question 14.2

The two-region geographical economics model predicts that manufacturing activity will spread over the two regions or agglomerate in one region depending on the size of three economic parameters:

- The (iceberg) transport cost (T)
- The elasticity of substitution (ε)
- The share of income spent on manufactures (δ_m)

A. Do high transport costs lead to spreading or agglomeration of manufacturing activity? Explain.

B. Does a high elasticity of substitution lead to spreading or agglomeration of manufacturing activity? Explain.

C. Does a high share of income spent on manufactures lead to spreading or agglomeration of manufacturing activity? Explain.

Question 14.3

Chapter 14 discusses the geographical economics model using graphs such as the one shown here.

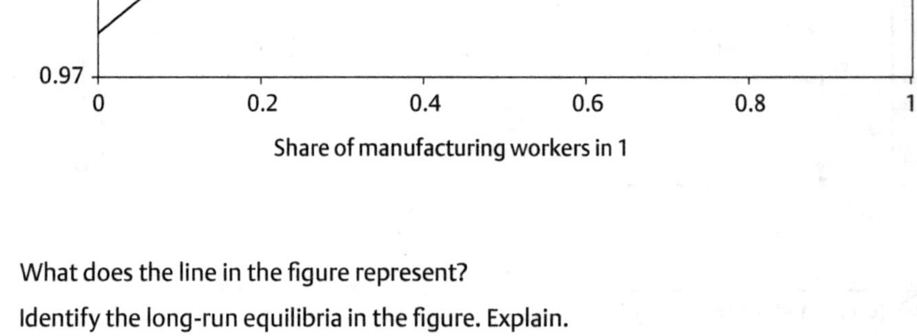

A. What does the line in the figure represent?

B. Identify the long-run equilibria in the figure. Explain.

C. How can you derive from the figure if a long-run equilibrium is stable or unstable?

D. Can you determine from the figure if manufacturing activity will agglomerate in the long run?

E. Draw a new figure, similar to the one shown here but based on a different parameter setting, in which the agglomeration of manufacturing firms is the only stable long-run equilibrium.

F. Draw a new figure, similar to the one shown here but based on a different parameter setting, in which the spreading of manufacturing firms is the only stable long-run equilibrium.

Question 14.4

This question reviews the general structure of the geographical economics model.

A. How do consumers decide how much to spend on food and manufacturing goods? What is the share of income they will spend on food?

B. Does every consumer spend an equal share of income on food? Why?

C. How do consumers decide on their consumption level for a particular variety of manufactures? What share of their income will they spend on one variety?

D. Is the wage rate for farmworkers necessarily equal between the two regions?

E. Is the wage rate for manufacturing workers necessarily equal between the two regions?

Question 14.5*

The geographical economics model differs in various ways from the models we have studied in earlier chapters of the book.

A. What is an equilibrium in the geographical economics model?

B. What is the difference between a long-run and a short-run equilibrium in the geographical economics model?

C. What are the endogenous variables of the geographical economics model?

D. With six equations and six endogenous variables it appears to be fairly easy to solve the model for Y_1 for example. Why is this not the case?

E. Why is a computer used to find the short-run equilibria?

Question 14.6

The analysis of the sustain points and the break point (see Figure 14.9) determines for which values of transport costs (T), elasticity of substitution (ε), and share of income spent on manufactures (δ_m) agglomeration, respectively spreading, is a stable long-run equilibrium.

A. What is a sustain point?

B. What is a break point?

C. Explain what the arrows in Figure 14.9 indicate.

D. Suppose that the elasticity of substitution ε is lower than in the base scenario depicted in Figure 14.9. How will this affect Figure 14.9 in your view? Why?

Question 14.7

Section 14.6 of the book analyses welfare in the geographical economics model.

A. How is welfare defined in this chapter?

A large part of the welfare analysis in section 14.6 is trying to determine if stability implies welfare maximization.

B. Why is this link between welfare and stability important?

C. What is the conclusion on the relationship between welfare and stability?

Empirical questions

Question 14.8

The importance of transport costs in international trade is empirically illustrated in Figure 14.3, depicting the relationship between German exports and distance to the export market. This question investigates if a similar relationship holds for Japan. The 'question 14-8' Excel file on the website contains data on Japanese exports, the distance to the export markets, and the size of these markets as measured by GDP.

A. Which countries comprise the top ten export markets for Japan? Does distance play a role in the export behaviour of Japan?

B. Calculate the natural logarithm of exports and of the distance to Japan. Run a regression on the results, using a constant and the distance to the Japanese market to estimate the size of the Japanese export flow. Illustrate your result in a graph. Does distance play a role in the export behaviour of Japan?

We will now correct for the size of the export market in this sample. To do this you have to estimate the following regression:

$$\ln(\text{export}) = A + B\ln(\text{GDP})$$

in which A is the intercept and B the slope of your linear regression model. After that you can calculate the adjusted exports as:

$$\ln(\text{adjusted export}) = \ln(\text{export}) - B\ln(\text{GDP})$$

C. Make a graph in which you put ln(adjusted export) on the vertical axis and ln(distance) on the horizontal axis. What can you conclude from this new figure?

Question 14.9

Section 14.2 discusses and illustrates the empirical regularity called Zipf's law. The 'question 14-9' Excel file on the website contains information for Argentina. Make a graph similar to Figure 14.2 for Argentina. Does Zipf's law hold for Argentina?

Question 14.10

Mainstream economists have paid relatively little attention to geographic factors for a long time, despite the fact that even a quick look at the distribution of income in the world (see Figure 1.3) suffices to see that geography (location) plays some role. On the web or in the library you can find a paper entitled 'Geography and economic development' by J. L. Gallup and J. D. Sachs with A. D. Mellinger.

A. What is the relationship between geography and economic growth according to the authors?

B. What is the implication of the analysis for the African nations?

C. What is the outlook for the future for the poorest nations on the planet according to the authors?

Question 14.11*

Locate on the web or in your library the paper called 'The location of European industry', written by K. H. Midelfart-Knarvik, H. G. Overman, S. J. Redding, and A. J. Venables. This empirical report describes the location and concentration of European industries. The answers to the questions below are given in the introduction to this paper.

A. Which economic theories are used in the report to explain the location of European industries?

B. The report compares the industrial structure of Europe and America. What does the report conclude? Can you explain this conclusion using the geographical economics model?

Simulation questions

Question 14.12

Chapter 14 analyses a two-region version of the geographical economics model. The 'racetrack economy' briefly described in the appendix to the Study Guide identifies more regions in a neutral, clock-like space. The 'question 14-12' Excel simulation on the website for this question uses (initially) a six-region racetrack economy. In the simulation you can change the transport costs and the initial distribution of manufacturing workers. After pushing a button the simulation calculates the new long-run equilibrium distribution of manufacturing workers over the six regions.

First, assume that the six regions are distributed as in the standard racetrack economy, see the figure below. This transport system is called scenario 1 in the simulation. The transport costs are $T = 1.5$. Assume that initially manufacturing workers are equally distributed among the six regions (you can fill in '$= 1/6$' in the simulation).

Scenario 1

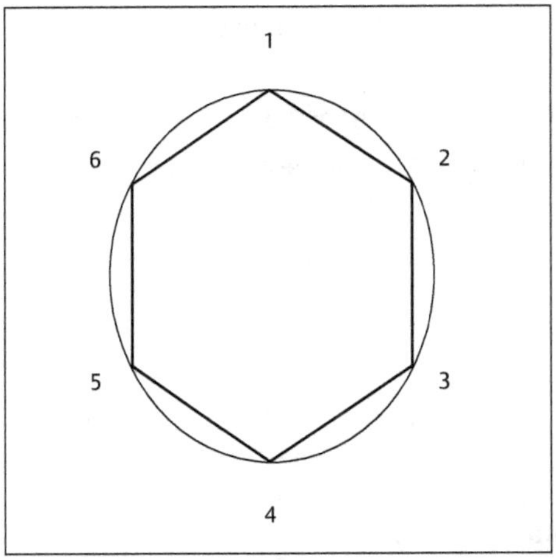

A. Is the initial distribution a long-run equilibrium? Why?

B. Experiment with small deviations in the initial distribution. Is the initial distribution a stable equilibrium in your view? Why?

C. Increase the transport costs and then repeat your experiments from question 14.12B. How does this affect your results?

Of course the distribution network of scenario 1 can be changed. You can experiment with such changes below. Before we start, return the transport costs to their old level. Suppose that the transport system changes to the structure shown in the figure below, called scenario 2 in the simulation. This time regions 2 and 5 are connected with each other using a kind of 'bridge', reducing the distance between them to one unit.

Scenario 2

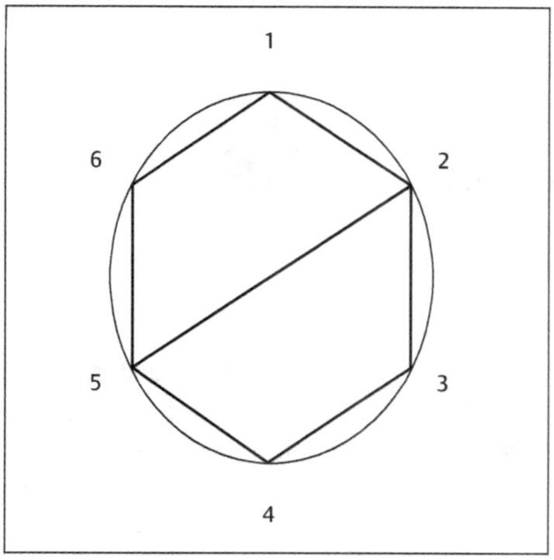

D. Assume that the manufacturing workers are initially equally distributed among the six regions. What is the long-run equilibrium of scenario 2?

E. Experiment with changes in the initial distribution of scenario 2. Is the long-run equilibrium from question 14.12D a stable equilibrium?

Scenario 3 below assumes that region 2 is well connected to the other regions.

Scenario 3

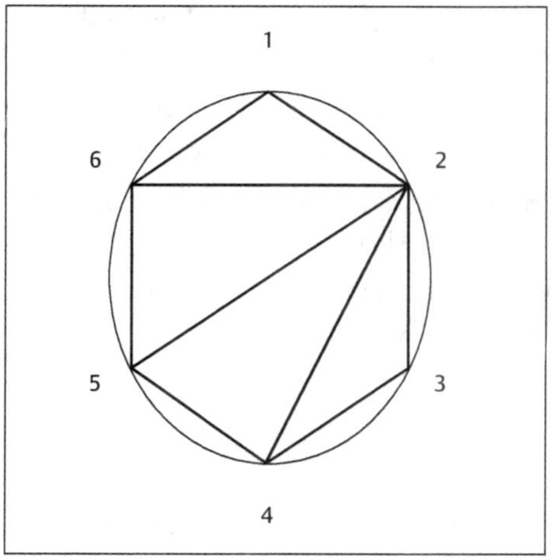

F. Assume again that the manufacturing workers are initially equally distributed among the six regions. What is the long-run equilibrium of scenario 3? Give an intuitive explanation of the results derived in this exercise.

15

Multinationals

Multinational firms, with increasing shares in world production, investment, and trade flows, represent the most visible part of the 'globalization' phenomenon. Chapter 15 evaluates some empirical evidence and analyses the economic forces underlying multinational firms.

Review questions

Question 15.1

Chapter 15 first describes some empirical observations on the investment flows between countries (foreign direct investment). The Markusen and Venables model (see section 15.5) explains some of the most important empirical observations. This question reviews the empirical observations and their theoretical explanations.

A. Are the FDI inflows into the least developed nations large or small? What is the theoretical explanation for this in the Markusen and Venables model?

B. Are the FDI inflows into the developed (OECD) nations large or small? What is the theoretical explanation for this in the Markusen and Venables model?

C. Are the FDI inflows into the middle-income countries large or small? What is the theoretical explanation for this in the Markusen and Venables model?

Question 15.2*

Several academics have wondered why a firm establishes a production plant abroad since this involves extra costs compared to home production (think, for example, of the cost of transferring people to a foreign country, of acquiring information, of overcoming language barriers, and coping with cultural differences).

A. What is required according to Dunning before firms establish or purchase production plants abroad? Describe all the conditions carefully.

B. Why do *all* conditions have to be satisfied before a firm becomes a multinational?

Question 15.3

Bicfun is a bicycle producing multinational firm with three production plants in three different countries. The Bicfun assembly plant is situated in country A, the Bicfun frame plant in country B, and the Bicfun parts plant in country C. The Bicfun frame plant produces a frame and the Bicfun parts plant a package of bicycle parts, both of which are then shipped to country A to be assembled in the Bicfun assembly plant, resulting in a complete bicycle which is sold on the market for 1,000 Euro.

The production cost of producing one bicycle frame in country B is 200 Euro. The production cost of the package of parts is 300 Euro. Assembling the bicycle in country A costs 50 Euro. The transfer price of frames and parts between the Bicfun plants may not deviate more than 50 Euro from the production price (the deviation can be either positive or negative). Otherwise the tax authorities of the different countries will suspect that Bicfun is evading their taxes and consequently give Bicfun a large fine. Countries A, B, and C levy different taxes on profits. The assembly plant in country A has to pay a 30 per cent tax on its profits, compared to a 40 per cent tax in country B, and a 20 per cent tax in country C. Furthermore, it is given that country A imposes a 10 per cent tariff on the value of imports coming into country A.

A. Calculate the optimal transfer price for a bicycle frame and a package of parts (the prices that the frame plant and parts plant demand from the assembly plant for their products) if it is assumed that the multinational strives for maximum profits. Denote only the local prices (without the tariffs).

B. What are the profits for every separate plant and what are the profits for the multinational as a whole?

Suppose that country A increases the import tariff to 15 per cent.

C. What are the optimal transfer prices in this case? Denote only the local price.

D. What is the profit of every separate plant and what is the profit of the multinational as a whole?

Question 15.4

Imagine a machine manufacturer operating in East Germany. Before the fall of the Berlin Wall the manufacturer is only producing for the national market and prohibited from exporting to other countries. After the fall of the Berlin Wall the manufacturer is allowed to sell machines to other countries. In contemplating how to deal with the new situation the manufacturer uses the model of Markusen and Venables.

A. At which node of the decision tree in Figure 15.8 is the manufacturer?

The manufacturer wants to sell the machines in four countries with the following characteristics:

- *West Germany* is more advanced and capital abundant compared to East Germany. Because both are neighbouring countries transport costs are low. Moreover, the German government provides a subsidy to East German firms establishing a plant in West Germany.

- *Poland* is also a neighbouring country with low transport costs. The Polish government does not provide a subsidy for the establishment of a plant. The level of development (measured by the endowment ratio) is more or less the same as in East Germany, but the Polish economy is considerably larger.
- As a result of newly introduced tariffs transport costs to the Czech Republic are very high. Like Poland, the Czech government does not provide a subsidy for the establishment of a new plant. East Germany and the Czech Republic are broadly equal in size and in level of development.
- *Slovakia* is not a neighbouring country, so transport costs are high. The establishment costs for a plant are high due to a tax. Also Slovakia and East Germany have the same level of development, but the Slovakian economy is smaller than the East German economy.

The manufacturer has to decide if he should establish a plant in the other country or produce the machines in East Germany and export the products.

B. Consider for each of the four countries if it is likely that the manufacturer establishes a new plant according to the Markusen and Venables model.

Question 15.5

A. The Markusen and Venables model distinguishes between two goods; food and manufactures. Multinationals may only arise in the production of manufactures and not in the production of food, such that the model focuses mainly on the manufacturing sector. Why is the food sector included in the model at all?

B. Figure 15.11, which summarizes the Markusen and Venables model, consists of squares. Is this a property of the model?

Empirical questions

Question 15.6

Chapter 15 of the book notes that relatively many international oriented companies are located in small developed countries. We will see if this is also true for companies active in the computer and office equipment industry. The 'question 15-6' Excel file on the website contains assets and sales data for 268 computer and office equipment companies in seventeen different countries. Devise a method to determine if the most international oriented companies are located in small developed countries.

Question 15.7

Determine for every (attempted) merger listed below if it is a horizontal, vertical, or conglomerate merger. Search the internet for information if necessary.

A. America Online and Time Warner

B. Vodafone Airtouch and Mannesmann

C. Honeywell and General Electric

D. ING-Group and Barings

E. Seagram and Polygram

F. Olivetti and Telecom Italia

Question 15.8

Try to find the working paper 'Internationalized production in world output' written by R. E. Lipsey, M. Blomström, and E. Ramstetter at the National Bureau of Economic Research (NBER). If your university or college has a licence you can download the paper from the NBER site (http://www.nber.org).

A. What is the objective of this paper?

B. Which methods (in this case measures) do the authors use?

C. What are the authors' conclusions?

16

New Goods, Growth and Development

Chapter 16 analyses economic growth and development using neoclassical models of capital accumulation, endogenous growth models stressing the role of profit seeking entrepreneurs for dynamic innovations, and the geography approach to explain the location of and large swings in economic prosperity.

Review questions

Question 16.1*

Chapter 16 starts with an introduction on new goods and how these have improved the standard of living.

A. How do economic researchers model the introduction of new goods?

B. Does the Solow growth model use one of the methods of question 16.1A?

C. Does the endogenous growth model discussed in the book use one of the methods of question 16.1A?

D. Does the geographical economics model discussed in the book use one of the methods of question 16.1A?

Question 16.2

Section 16.4 discusses the Solow model, which forms the starting point of economic growth theory. The central equation of the model is given by: $sAk_t^{\alpha} = (\mu + n)k_t$. This equation defines the steady-state equilibrium of the model.

A. What is a steady-state equilibrium?

B. What happens to output per capita if the capital–labour ratio is constant in the Solow model for a constant level of technology?

The graph for question 16.2 depicts the left-hand side and the right-hand side of equation 16.3.

C. What is measured on the vertical axis of the diagram?

D. Draw the effect of an increase in the population growth rate n in the graph. What happens to the steady-state equilibrium and why?

E. Draw the effect of an increase in the savings rate s in the graph. What happens to the steady-state equilibrium and why?

F. What does a constant state of technology in the Solow model imply for the output level per capita?

G. How can the Solow model describe the empirical facts of economic growth?

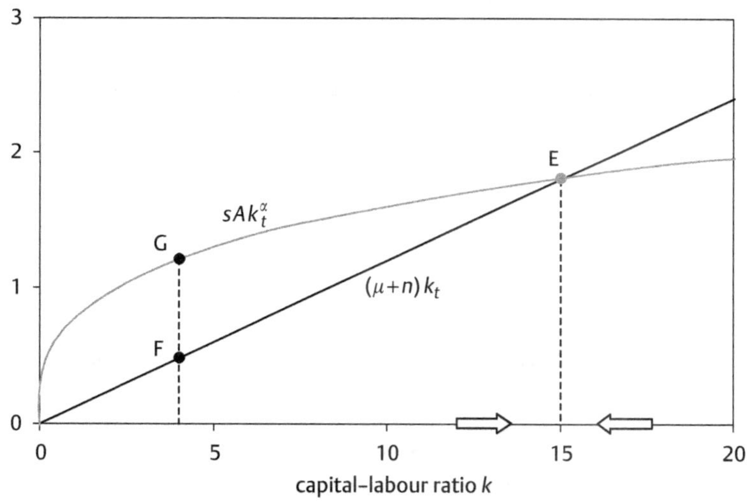

Question 16.3

Section 16.6 of the book discusses the structure and implications of the endogenous growth model.

A. What is the main difference between this growth theory and that of Solow?

B. What seems to be the key factor for a growing income per capita if you look at these two classes of growth models?

In the endogenous growth model, the rate of innovation in the economy is determined within the model. The explicit solution, derived in the technical notes to Chapter 16, is:

$$1+g=\frac{F}{(1+\theta)(F-L/\varepsilon)},$$

where g is the rate of innovation, F is a parameter for the fixed cost of inventing a new variety, L is the labour force, θ is the rate of time preference, and ε is the elasticity of substitution between varieties.

C. Based on the above equation determine what happens to the rate of innovation if:

- F, the fixed cost of inventing a new variety, increases
- L, the labour force, increases
- θ, the rate of time preference, increases.

D. Based on your knowledge of the structure of the endogenous growth model, explain intuitively why each of the effects in question 16.3C arises.

The United States government has launched a series of investigations into the abuse of market power by Microsoft, a producer of computer software. The company claims that its market power actually benefits its customers, as it is the best way to fulfil their needs.

E. Explain how the endogenous growth model is related to the discussion of the Microsoft case.

Question 16.4

Section 16.7 of the book evaluates the outcome of a number of computer simulations for the racetrack economy (see the appendix to this Study Guide) of the geographical economics model, introducing congestion costs to mitigate the economic powers of agglomeration.

A. Explain why the endogenous growth model and the Solow model cannot explain the empirically observed large swings in prosperity.

B. Explain how the experiment in section 16.7 results in large swings in prosperity.

C. If we use the simulation results on the distribution of income for the world today, with very high transport costs in earlier times and rapidly dropping transport cost now, what does this imply for the future?

The simulations of section 16.7 illustrate the snowball effect of economic forces, for example by showing that the clustering of firms in a region as a result of increasing returns to scale make this region attractive for other firms in surrounding regions.

D What does the above comment imply for the development of Africa? Do you think that there is a link with the 'brain drain' phenomenon?

Empirical questions

Question 16.5

The theory of economic growth increasingly focuses on technological development and knowledge but how do we measure these? One approach is to look at the number of patents filed over a certain time period. The 'question 16-5' Excel file on the website contains data on the number of patents applied for at the Dutch patent office, ranging from 1981 to 1997 and subdivided according to the country of origin.

A. Which twenty countries apply for most patents in the Netherlands? Make a ranking for both 1981 and 1997.

B. What is the position of the United States in this ranking in 1981 and 1997? Can you explain the change?

C. Plot the number of patent applications from Norway and Finland from 1981 to 1997 in a graph. Can you explain the different developments?

D. Plot the number of patent applications from Spain and Portugal from 1981 to 1997 in a graph. Can you explain the developments?

Question 16.6

In the 'question 16-6' Excel file on the website we have collected the necessary information for calculating the Solow residual. As you can see in equation 16.4, this requires knowledge on changes in the stocks of capital and labour and knowledge on the parameter alpha, for which we take the average investment share of GDP over the years in the data set.

A. Calculate the Solow residual for all countries in the data set. Is the Solow residual 'large' in your opinion?

B. Choose one country for which you plot the actual growth rate and the Solow residual in a graph.

In the 1990s there was a discussion on the per capita growth performance of the Asian countries in the data set. It was claimed that capital accumulation was the main contributor to economic growth. Changes in the technology parameter A (often called total factor productivity in the literature) seemed to have had a small impact. This spelled bad news for the future of the Asian economies, which gave rise to a debate on the low total factor productivity of Asian nations.

C. Do you think that the way we measure changes in A (total factor productivity) gives us an accurate picture of economic developments? Explain.

D. Can you find evidence in the data set to substantiate the claim above that most per capita growth in Asia is the result of capital accumulation?

Question 16.7

Try to find the paper 'It's not factor accumulation: stylised facts and growth models' by W. Easterly and R. Levine on the web or in your library. The paper uses the term total factor productivity (TFP) for the technology parameter A in the book.

A. What stylized facts do the authors extract from their empirical research?

B. What is the role of capital accumulation for growth according to the authors?

C. What role does TFP play in explaining differences in growth rates across nations?

D. Do you see a role for the geographical economics model in creating a better understanding of the differences in economic growth detected by the authors? Explain.

Technical questions

Question 16.8

A large part of Chapter 16 focuses on economic growth theory, which started with the Solow model of economic growth. As described in section 16.4, the Solow model eventually evolves towards a steady state, where the economy follows a so-called balanced growth path.

A. At the balanced growth path, what is the growth rate of capital? And of output per capita?

B. Determine the steady-state value of the capital–labour ratio, and of output per capita.

C. Now define $k = K/AL, y = Y/AL$ and let A grow at a constant rate g. How does this affect your answers to questions 16.8A and 16.8B?

17

Applied Trade Policy Modelling

Chapter 17 briefly evaluates some of the problems and procedures of applied trade policy modelling for demand and supply in a partial equilibrium and general equilibrium framework. It also discusses the problem of measuring the hidden costs of trade restrictions.

Review questions

Question 17.1

A. What is demand bias?

B. Use a graph to explain how demand bias may invalidate the Heckscher-Ohlin result.

C. Can demand bias explain the Leontief paradox?

Question 17.2

In section 17.2 the Armington utility function for two countries was introduced. For country 1 this Armington utility function is given by:

$$U_1 = (a_{11}x_1^{\rho} + a_{21}x_2^{\rho})^{1/\rho}; \quad 0 < \rho < 1$$

A. What is the Armington assumption?

B. Why is this assumption made in applied trade policy modelling?

C. What does the Armington utility function of country 2 look like? Write down the equation.

D. What does the utility function of country 1 look like if there are three countries?

Question 17.3

In March 2001 some of the world's largest pharmaceutical companies brought the South African government before the High Court in Pretoria. Their complaint was that the Medicines Act, which had not come into effect at that time, would undermine the patent rules of the World Trade Organization. An important part of the dispute was the provision that allowed for the parallel imports of patented AIDS medicines from other countries where these medicines are sold at a lower price.

We can analyse this court case using the following data for the market of AIDS medicines in South Africa.[1]

Number of medicines currently sold in South Africa	1,000,000
Current price of the medicine in South Africa	US$ 9.34
Price of the medicine in Thailand	US$ 0.60

Initially South African AIDS patients have to buy their medicines from the large pharmaceutical companies for US$ 9.34. If the Medicines Act is activated, cheaper medicines can be imported from Thailand, such that the price drops to US$ 0.60.

Assume that the demand for AIDS medicines in South Africa is given by:

$$p = a - bQ$$

where p is the price for the medicine, Q the quantity demanded, and a and b are parameters. Normally when conducting a policy study, one has to estimate this demand function. As this is beyond the scope of this question we quantify the demand function in a non-rigorous way.

A. What would be a reasonable value for the constant 'b'? Explain your choice.

B. Using the value for 'b' from question 17.3A, what is the value of the constant 'a' in the demand function?

We have now gathered and estimated all the necessary data to begin the analysis.

C. Draw the demand function for AIDS medicines in South Africa. Draw the change in welfare if the South African government passes the Medicines Act in the same figure.

D. Indicate the Dupuit triangle in the figure.

E. What are the dynamic problems arising from the introduction of the Medicines Act?

F. Do you advise the South African government to introduce the Medicines Act or not? Why?

Question 17.4

A Kenyan tractor producer is considering introducing a new type of tractor. Some Kenyan farmers would like to buy the tractor as it incorporates new features. The tractor producer is facing the demand curve for his new tractor as shown in the figure opposite.

[1] The prices are in fact the real prices of a certain AIDS medicine in South Africa and Thailand.

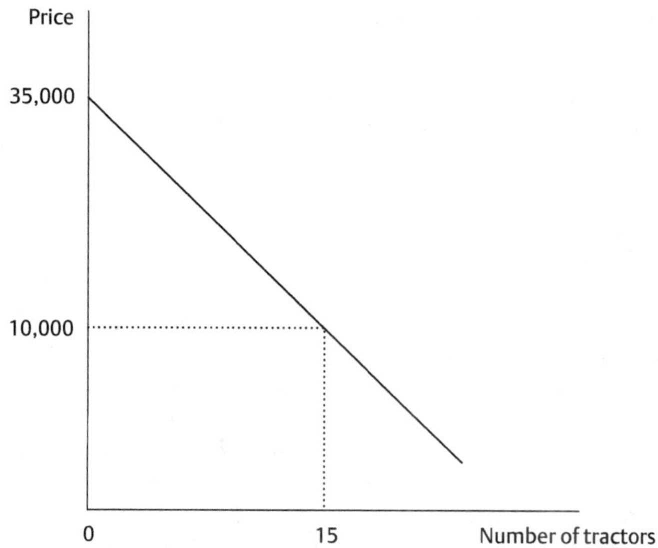

The development cost for the new type of tractor is 80,000 Euro. After its introduction the new tractor can be produced for 10,000 Euro a piece.

A. Assume that Kenya is in autarky. Will the Kenyan tractor producer develop and sell the new type of tractor? Explain.

B. Is it sensible for the Kenyan government to finance the development of the new type of tractor?

Now assume that Kenya can trade freely with its neighbour Tanzania, where there is also demand for the new tractor as given by the demand curve in the figure below. There is however no producer who could possibly develop this new type of tractor.

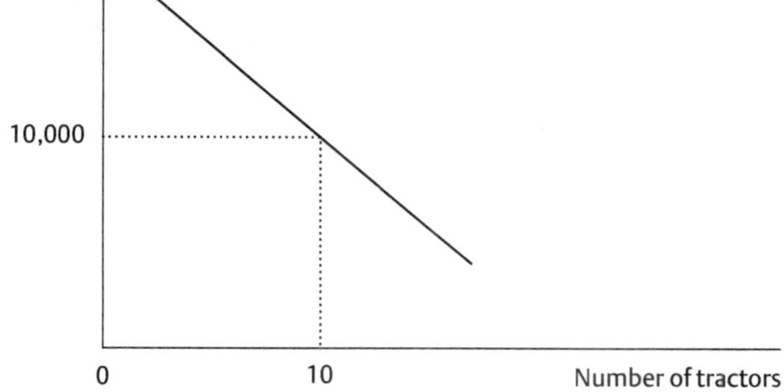

C. Will the Kenyan tractor producer develop and sell the new type of tractor in Kenya and Tanzania?

D. Is it sensible for the Kenyan government to finance the development of the new type of tractor if trade with Tanzania can take place?

Question 17.5

The paper by Cattaneo et al. (1999) entitled 'Costa Rica trade liberalization, fiscal imbalances, and macroeconomic policy' is an example of a study that tries to resolve a policy issue by using a computable general equilibrium model. Since trade liberalization in Costa Rica leads to a loss in tax revenue the question arises how the government of Costa Rica can compensate this revenue loss. Three possible solutions are proposed, namely (i) decrease government expenditures, (ii) increase the enterprise tax, or (iii) increase the sales tax.[2] Using a general equilibrium model, the authors try to assess the consequences of these different policy options. The table shows the results for Costa Rica as a whole and for its most important sectors.

Costa Rica under different policies (% change from base)

	Change government expenditure	Change enterprise tax	Change sales tax
Real value added			
Bananas	−1.80	0.12	4.81
Coffee	7.49	11.85	13.10
Livestock	2.88	−1.01	−4.12
Fish & forestry	−0.91	−1.08	0.71
Construction	−26.69	−6.65	−1.61
Total	0.16	0.15	0.07
Imports			
Bananas	0.00	0.00	0.00
Coffee	0.00	0.00	0.00
Livestock	0.57	−6.18	−9.95
Fish & forestry	−2.93	−6.56	−8.14
Construction	0.00	0.00	0.00
Total	5.51	6.96	7.39
Exports			
Bananas	−1.91	0.04	4.71
Coffee	0.00	0.00	0.00
Livestock	5.21	4.37	1.99
Fish & forestry	0.30	2.27	6.23
Construction	0.00	0.00	0.00
Total	5.59	7.06	7.49

Source: Cattaneo *et al.* (1999).

[2] The policy variables are changed in such a way that the government budget is balanced.

A. Which policy should the government of Costa Rica pursue in your opinion to best serve the interests of the economy as a whole.

B. Which policy should the government of Costa Rica pursue in your opinion if it only wants to serve the interests of a specific sector.

C. Which policy option will the government of Costa Rica choose in your opinion?

Empirical questions

Question 17.6

We want to analyse if the Linder hypothesis holds for the trade between Italy and different regions. The table shows the Grubel–Lloyd index for some industries.

Grubel–Lloyd index for trade between Italy and different regions, 1995

	Africa	EU	Latin America	NAFTA	North-East Asia	South Asia
Food and live animals	14.2	37.4	4.0	16.5	25.5	1.6
Beverages and tobacco	20.9	46.3	23.2	9.9	9.5	0.1
Crude materials	24.1	41.9	10.9	9.1	33.7	15.6
Mineral fuels	12.5	54.7	35.4	25.3	25.8	2.8
Animal, vegetable oil, fat	17.1	75.9	42.0	2.9	3.5	1.8
Chemicals	16.3	75.6	39.3	72.8	68.2	49.8
Basic manufactures	41.8	63.1	28.4	34.5	39.2	23.4
Machines, transport equipment	4.8	76.2	14.2	56.4	58.8	12.7

Source: NAPES website, http://napes.anu.edu.au/

A. What does the Linder hypothesis predict about trade between two developed countries?

B. What does the Linder hypothesis predict about trade between a developed and a less developed country?

C. Do the data in the table support the Linder hypothesis in your view?

Simulation questions

Question 17.7

Devarajan *et al.* (1997) provide an introduction into economic simulations by presenting a computable general equilibrium model of the economy of Sri Lanka. The 'question 17-7' Excel file on the website is based on this model and allows you to analyse the consequences of policy changes.

Suppose that the just-elected president of Sri Lanka promised during the election campaign that he would increase real consumption by 2 per cent during his term. He is trying to decide which tax instrument to use for this goal. As an adviser, you are asked to analyse the different options using the model in the Excel file.

The starting values of the simulation are indicated in the simulation itself under the heading 'base'.

A. Try to determine if the import tariff should be increased or decreased in order to raise real consumption. Do the same for the export duty, the value added tax and the income tax.

B. Make three different scenarios (combinations of tax rates) which will increase the real consumption by 2 per cent.

C. What are the consequences of these tax changes for the economy of Sri Lanka?

D. What will your advice to the president be? Explain.

Appendix

The Racetrack Economy: Many Locations in Neutral Space

The analysis in Chapter 14 of the book focuses on the two-region geographical economics model. However, the approach holds quite generally if we identify an arbitrary number R of locations, as long as we specify the distances D_{rs} between all locations r and s, such that we can calculate $T_{rs} = T^{D_{rs}}$, and know the production level ϕ_r of the immobile activity in each location r. The main advantage of the two-region model is that 'space' is inherently neutral. Neither location is preferred by construction over the other location, because the distance between the two locations is the same, and hence so are the transport costs. Any endogenous location pattern, such as agglomeration or spreading, arising in the two-region model is therefore a consequence of the structure of the economic interactions between agents within the model, and not the result of some pre-imposed geographic structure favouring economic activity in a particular location.

To preserve the neutrality of space in a many-location setting it is useful to analyse a simple geometry, in which the locations are evenly distributed in a circle with transportation only possible along the rim of that circle, known as 'the racetrack economy'. Its structure is quite simple, as illustrated in Figure A.1. The R locations are equally and sequentially spaced around the circumference of a circle, with location R next to location 1, as in a clock. The distance between any two adjacent locations is 1, such that the transport costs between adjacent locations is T. The distance between any two arbitrary locations is the length of the shortest route along the circumference of the circle. We assume that the immobile production is evenly distributed among all locations.

Panel (*a*) of Figure A.1 illustrates the racetrack economy if there are 3 locations. The distance between all locations is 1, since they are all adjacent to one another. Panel (*b*) illustrates the racetrack economy if there are 5 locations. The distance from location 1 to locations 2 and 5 is 1, because these are adjacent locations, and the distance from location 1 to locations 3 and 4 is 2, because it requires 2 steps from location 1 to reach either location. Similarly, panel (*c*) illustrates the racetrack economy if there are 12 locations, where, for example, the distance from location 1 to locations 5 and 9 is 4, as both locations require 4 steps to be reached from location 1.

Panels (*d*) and (*e*) of Figure A.1 show a typical simulation run for the racetrack economy with 12 locations.[1] The simulation procedure is as follows.

1. Start with an initial, randomly chosen, distribution of the manufacturing labour force.
2. Determine the short-run equilibrium, given this initial distribution, using the iterative procedure described in section 14.5 of the book.
3. Calculate the real wage in the short-run equilibrium for all locations.
4. Redistribute the manufacturing workforce across the locations, moving labourers towards locations with high real wages and away from locations with low real wages; it is possible at

[1] The parameters for Figure A.1 (*d*) and (*e*) are: $\delta_{\mathrm{m}} = 0.4$; $\varepsilon = 5$; $T = 1.25$.

Figure A.1 The racetrack economy; number of locations = R

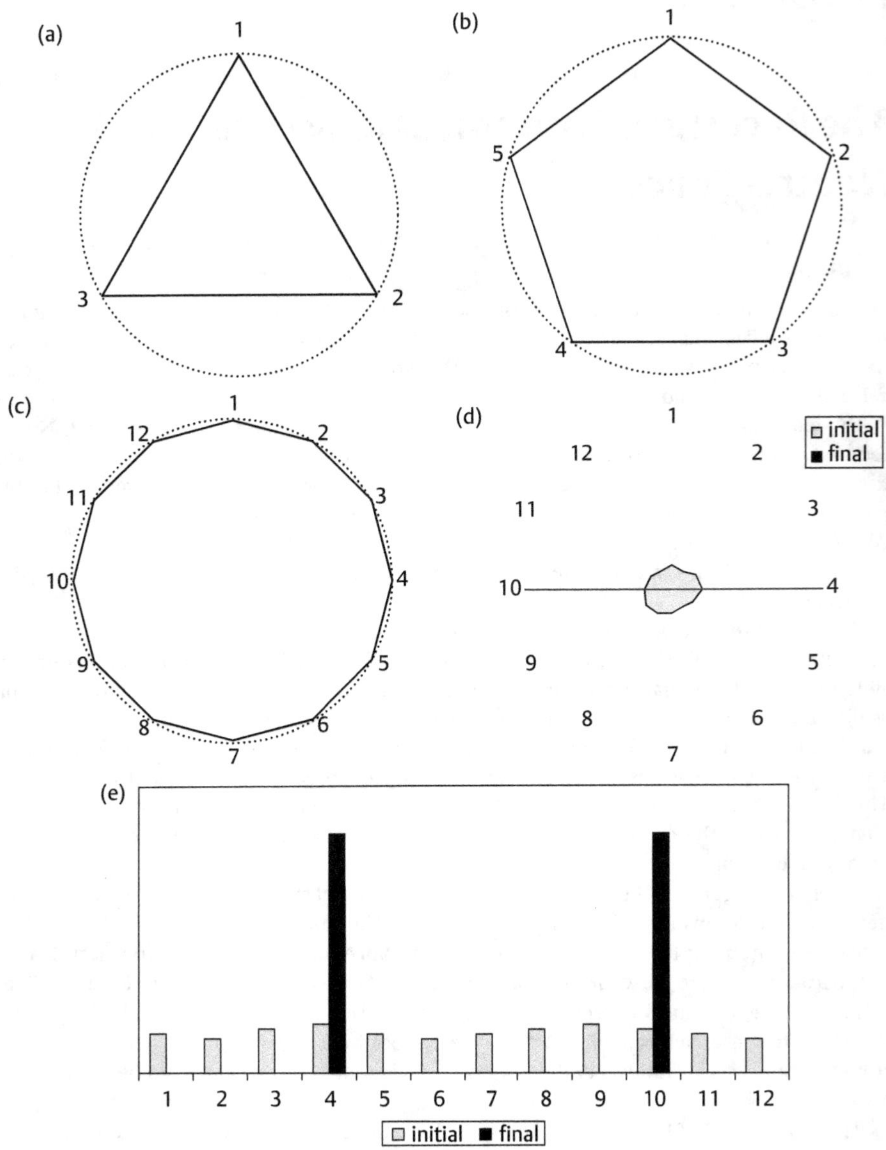

this stage that a location stops producing manufacturing goods because there are no more manufacturing workers.

5. Repeat steps 2–4 until a long-run equilibrium is reached in step 3; that is until the real wage is equal in all locations with a positive manufacturing labour force, or until all manufacturing labour is agglomerated in only one location.

Panel (*d*) in Figure A.1 illustrates the simulation run using the same graphical approach as panels (*a*)–(*c*). Apparently, all manufacturing production eventually ends up in only two cities, namely locations 4 and 10, exactly opposite to one another. Both locations produce exactly half of the manufacturing varieties. Panel (*e*) shows the same simulation run using a column chart of the initial and final distribution of manufacturing production. The cities 4 and 10, which eventually emerge from the simulation as the only locations with manufacturing production were already large initially, which allowed them to grow. Initial size is, however, not the only determining force for the long-run equilibrium. This is demonstrated by location 9, which initially is slightly larger than location 10, but eventually disappears as it is too close to location 4.

If we repeat the simulation with the 12-location racetrack economy for a different randomly chosen initial distribution of the manufacturing workforce, and for different parameter values, it turns out that the outcome depicted in Figure A.1 panels (*d*) and (*e*) is quite typical. Usually, all manufacturing production is eventually agglomerated in only 1 or 2 cities. If there are 2 cities, they are equal in size and opposite of one another (but these are, of course, not always in locations 4 and 10). All other locations eventually do not produce any manufacturing goods.

Question 14.12 in this Study Guide asks you to experiment with the parameter settings of the model in the racetrack economy using the Excel simulation available on the website. Moreover, this simulation allows you to perform some simple policy experiments in a setting with non-neutral space.

References

CATTANEO, A., HINOJOSA-OJEDA, R. A., and ROBINSON, S. (1999), 'Costa Rica trade liberalization, fiscal imbalances, and macroeconomic policy: a computable general equilibrium model', *North American Journal of Economics and Finance*, 10: 39–67.

DEVARAJAN, S., GO, D. S., LEWIS, J. D., ROBINSON, S., and SINKO, P. (1997), 'Simple general equilibrium modeling', in J. F. Francois and K. A. Reinert (eds.), *Applied Methods for Trade Policy Analysis*, Cambridge: Cambridge University Press: 156–85.

MARREWIJK, C. VAN (2002), *International Trade and the World Economy*, Oxford: Oxford University Press.

OTTENS, D. (2000), 'Revealed Comparative Advantage: An Empirical Analysis', unpublished Masters thesis, Erasmus University, Rotterdam.

The manufacturer's authorised representative in the EU for product safety is Oxford University Press España S.A. of el Parque Empresarial San Fernando de Henares, Avenida de Castilla, 2 – 28830 Madrid (www.oup.es/en or product.safety@oup.com). OUP España S.A. also acts as importer into Spain of products made by the manufacturer.

www.ingramcontent.com/pod-product-compliance
Lightning Source LLC
LaVergne TN
LVHW022106200926
848481LV00003B/1075
* 9 7 8 0 1 9 9 2 5 3 1 4 2 *